DROWNING IN THE LIGHT

DROWNING IN THE LIGHT

MEMORIES OF THE NEW AGE

I.J. ROSEN

Copyright © 2016
I.J. Rosen

I dedicate this book to my father Laurence S. Rosen for bringing Light into my world.
I dedicate this book to my mother Ruth Rosen for inspiring me to make art.

CONTENTS

Acknowledgments · viii
Prologue: Asleep Under Water· ix

Chapter One: Spiritual Electricity· 1
Chapter Two: Initiation — Children Of The Sun · · · · · · · · · · · 21
Chapter Three: The Science Of Transfiguration· · · · · · · · · · · · 35
Chapter Four: Cabin In Elk · 49
Chapter Five: Galisteo Basin · 57
Chapter Six: Superconductive · 67
Chapter Seven: Dark Mirror · 76
Chapter Eight: 2012—End Of The New Age · · · · · · · · · · · · · 88

About The Author · 108

ACKNOWLEDGMENTS

I want to acknowledge every individual that has been woven into my story in this book, whether you pushed me to look at my own shadow or reminded me that I am Light.

To my wife Deena for always being by my side and showing me the path of love—you are my Angel forever.

To the first two people that read this book:

My daughter Kylea, who grew up with my story telling and continues to inspire me to live my life as an artist.

My agent Bill Gladstone, to whom I sent this manuscript with no expectation and was blown away by his true excitement and dedication to see this published.

To the Waterside team that made this happen. Johanna Maaghul for ongoing support. Kenneth Kales for superb editing. Richard Del Maestro for bringing out the best in me in recording the audiobook. Darlene Swanson for being able to take my visualization and turn it into a cover design. Chris Van Buren for being the awesome marketing strategist you are.

To my sister, Elyssa Rosen, for always being a phone call away during the dark nights of my soul and to Richard Savage for our daily walks around the creek and stimulating conversation.

PROLOGUE: ASLEEP UNDER WATER

"Letting the days go by... let the water hold me down"
—Talking Heads

The Electromagnetic Sea

When you are at the ocean walking along the shore with the sun setting behind you—all you will see in front of you is your shadow. If you turn and face the sun there is no shadow, only Light!

Just to put things in metaphysical perspective, the Earth moves through 2,000 year astrological cycles placing anyone reading this book at the cusp of the Piscean/Aquarian Age. The symbol of the Piscean Age is the fish—we have been bottom crawlers on the sea of electromagnetism, wondering if there is a sky above the surface with a Father on a Throne. The fish is also the symbol of Christ who ascended from the dense, dark waters of this electromagnetic sea only to reappear as a body of Light.

New Age folks have adapted the concept of "ascension" to fit their cosmology —Galactic Federation leaders coming to our planet as emissaries to lead us into an age of "peace on Earth."

This is no different from the Christian belief of salvation. Christ coming back to rule the worthy in a paradise where lions and lambs are hanging together. Either through the final days in the Book of Revelation or New Age beliefs in Mayan prophecies and UFO evacuations—they are all pointing to some "Omega Point" or end time rapture-like event—some anomalous space-time overlap with higher beings that will accelerate our evolution out of primitive technological existence and save us from total destruction.

We in the modern world have achieved so much in our material wealth but remain mostly spiritually impoverished. All the suffering in the world is a result of the delusion of separation. The belief that Creator is separate from Creation fosters a feeling of abandonment and judgment creating "God-fearing" people not only scared of their own shadows but also scared of their own Light.

We are truly made of liquid Light! Our bodies are composed of cells. Each cell is filled with cytoplasmic fluid. We are liquid and we carry the electromagnetic waves of the world inside of us. Just like it was in the womb, we are floating in an ocean of consciousness in which we shape our world experience. This is why it is important to learn to flow with life. And this is my story that begins at birth and almost ends in death. But you have to read this book to understand what it means to be "Drowning in the Light."

CHAPTER ONE: SPIRITUAL ELECTRICITY

"Music is the electrical soil in which the spirit lives thinks and invents."

—Ludwig van Beethoven

Kundalini Rising

Born into the rubber-gloved hands of a masked doctor, my memory of Heaven washed away in the sterile fluorescent-lit electric light of the 1950's Brooklyn hospital room. When I was able to speak, I asked my mother where I came from. She said I came from the stork, from the sky. My first home was on Kings Highway in Brooklyn. Our building was across the street from a hospital. I used to look out the window, gazing toward the heavens, watching for babies descending through the hospital roof into soft cushy blankets at their mother's side.

My earliest memory goes back to the crib. I remember lying in the crib, watching the illuminated dust particles floating in the beam of light coming through the partially opened Venetian blinds. The dust particles looked so familiar, like galaxies of stars floating through space. I had descended from the heavens, and like the dust particles, I landed on this surface called earth.

My father was a lighting fixture salesman. He always had shiny metal things—cool pieces of brass and crystals for the chandeliers. When he took me to the showrooms, I was immersed in a sea of electric light. Dazzling, scintillating light! I loved turning the dimmer dial down and watching the light become faint like the setting sun, only to turn the dial up again, watching the filament light up in each bulb, bursting forth like the rising sun. I was fascinated by light.

I was equally fascinated with electricity. To think that this invisible energy practically ran the world. I somehow sort of figured that I, too, had electricity inside of me—perhaps an awareness of my soul? Was the soul like a filament of a bulb? The soul touches spirit like the filament touches electricity. Was there something behind everything, animating everything with life—some sort of etheric self-organizing field—a field that interfaces with an electromagnetic body? Spiritual voltage?

Dimly lit souls will spend their lives suffering because they are afraid to turn up the juice: their spiritual electricity. When they get in touch with their soul, they consciously tap the spiritual current that fills the universe. This Light of the universe is an inner Light that radiates out to all the corners of self.

Your picture will be clear without any interference. Our bodies are like television sets filled with tubes and circuitry. We are bioelectrical beings: mitochondrion transistors and microtubule cellular fiber optics. Your DNA antenna receives your soul's broadcast. When you die, the tube goes black, but the story is still being broadcast. The story exists in waves on the electromagnetic sea.

Perhaps television was a facsimile of the inner architecture of life?

As far back as I can remember I was fascinated with the television. Refraining from asking my mother how the people got into the TV, I decided to trace the pathway. How could Mighty

Mouse and Howdy Doody get into the TV through such a narrow wire? I traced the wire to the wall socket, and when I pulled the wire out of the wall, Howdy Doody, Tinkerbell and the entire entourage disappeared into a black screen. Aha! They must have entered through these slits in the wall socket. There on the table was a hairpin, the perfect size to fit into the slit. I poked the pin into the slit. Shocked— it was my first taste of electricity! A taste I would never forget! All I can remember was that I literally saw stars. A brilliant multitude of stars! Had I been thrust out of my body into the celestial realm?

Sometime after that, I began a relationship with an invisible friend. I called him "Green Boy." Green Boy had green-colored skin, a big head with big eyes, pointed ears and a small body. He looked something like a cross between an elf and E.T., maybe an elemental nature spirit or some kind of fairy. He usually appeared when I was in a hypnogogic state—the state of consciousness between waking and sleeping.

Gravitationally Trapped Light

In 1960, we packed up our blue Plymouth De Soto and moved to the suburbs. That was the last I saw of Green Boy. I entered the world of cookie-cutter homes and chemically fertilized lawns. The suburbs were a sort of upside down world where you parked on the driveway and drove on the parkway, and practically nobody walked on the sidewalks. When the sun went down in the evening, you could see the blue glow of a television set in each living room as families sat and watched the lives of fictitious families served by Aunt Jemima, Uncle Ben and other stereotypical black servants invented by the white men of Madison Avenue.

Going to school every day, I daydreamed my way through the schoolyard. In the classroom, sitting still in the little wooden desk was a great challenge for me. I pressed the palm of my hands into my eye sockets and would see stars all around. Seriously, try this! Press your palms into your eye sockets—not too hard. Everything will become black and then you will see stars. I had learned how to literally "space out." Well, until I heard the familiar voice of my teacher saying, "Wake up and come back to Earth." If only Mr. Dubman knew that I was actually far away from Earth. If he only knew that the universe is made of Light and is at the heart of every particle of existence.

Somehow, I thought I knew more about science than anybody else. I knew that there was a unified field. I always had the notion that there was a substance-like glue that held everything together—that we were like alphabets of matter in some starry soup, or pieces of fruit in a quantum Jello mold.

Stars were everywhere! Even in the speckled linoleum tiles. Everything was made of stars. The patterns were everywhere. Everything was swirling like galaxies and soft serve ice cream. Everything was like a snowflake, a one of a kind electromagnetic signature. It's amazing that no two people share the same fingerprint. We are all unique electromagnetic waves in an infinite universal ocean. I knew this deep inside me.

And yet, I could not learn how to subtract. I failed math and was left back in first grade. I overheard my mother talking to the teacher when they agreed it would be best to have me repeat first grade. I began to think I was dumb. I began to lose my memory of the stars in everything. And spacing out was getting harder as I increasingly felt a responsibility to work the left hemisphere of my brain. The feeling of being gravitationally trapped Light was like the fear of being trapped in a normal life. All I could see in my future was *GI Joe* or *Father Knows Best*.

And then I heard *Anthem of The Sun* by The Grateful Dead. I was twelve years old and it was 1968. A new world of psychedelic culture emerged in my universe. I feared that I would be drafted into the Vietnam War: this inspired me to become more focused in school. I discovered that my great talent was that of an artist. I loved to design record covers. I would make up names for groups and create album covers. I knew this was what I wanted to do when I grew up.

When I was fourteen years old, I inherited my family's old portable black and white television set. After I said goodnight and turned out the light in my bedroom, I had my little ritual. I discovered that if I set the TV dial between stations, I could create "TV snow." I turned the brightness down and the contrast up. The television screen gave the appearance of stars moving through the blackness of space. I put on some good space music and donned my headphones. With Pink Floyd's *Set the Controls to the Heart of the Sun*, I journeyed far away from my suburban split-level reality, adrift on an ocean of Light waves. No longer imprisoned by time and space. No longer feeling like gravitationally trapped Light.

Though I had little interest in science books and left-brain learning, I knew things about the universe. I knew that, to some extent, I was nothing but Light dressed up as matter! I began to see how nothing is the source of everything, and I wondered if one day we would all wake up to the fact that matter is a dream. That matter is a shadow of the mind. That God is like the Wizard of Oz behind the curtain! That it is all a projection!

Life As A Movie

I loved going to the movies. I was thrilled when the curtain rolled back and light splashed onto the screen. I loved to observe the beam of light that shone down from the projection booth. It was magical that this one beam of light was creating a world upon a blank white screen—all that color and motion radiating forth from one single bulb. One filament touches the infinite flow of electricity and illuminates an entire theatre. The movie screen acts like the matrix. It organizes the light projected onto it into a story of moving pictures, like frames of time moving through the void of space—a grand archetypal drama working itself out in light and shadow.

I began to understand that, to some degree, I could direct the movie of my life in my head and that the universe would rearrange itself to out-picture my daydreaming. As a teenager, I stood in front of the mirror with my air guitar, wearing my mother's scarf around my head like Jimi Hendrix. I would enter the mirror and I would be in an underground club. I was in a movie in my mind; I actually could see and feel myself in a parallel reality.

In 1974 I was studying fine arts at Boston University and was disillusioned with the traditional academic fine art approach of "paint the still life and draw the nude models." Besides Howard Zinn's history class in which I learned the untold history of the U.S., I lived for my art history class. As soon as the instructor turned off the light and projected the slide—I could step into the painting. I was realizing I had a sort of sixth sense and could feel the emotion of the artist through their work.

I knew I was born to be an artist. I lamented for the days of artists gathering in the local café, sharing ideas about existence and abstractions. I wanted to wear paint-splattered jeans and be identified as an artist to the tourists on the tour bus. I knew there was only one path to follow—my heart. All my sketches of the nude models looked like extraterrestrials. I did not fit in the traditional art world. I wanted the real art world. I wanted New York. To be hanging out with other artists and musicians, expressing my soul.

In my movie, no one understood me. I am an enigma, but still fascinating. In my movie, I am a revolutionary artist—the galvanizer of an art movement and someone who would be recognized in the history of the era. It is amazing how powerful the ego truly is!

Alien Art World

By the time I reached my twenties, I was living in a turn-of-the-century building in the SoHo section of New York City. Here, I, in the midst of a pulsating art world, needed to make my mark, to channel this intensity—the surging spiritual electricity that had sat dormant through my suburban childhood.

In the late 70s, lower Manhattan was a thriving culture of underground arts. In 1978, I spent many a day sitting on a stoop on the corner of Spring Street and West Broadway, in the shadow of the Twin Towers, playing minimalist music on a battery-powered Electro-Harmonix synthesizer. Inspired by such legendary musicians as Phillip Glass, Terry Riley and John Cage, I repeated a sequence of notes. My fingers merged with the touch-sensitive keypad, creating an alien-like sound, as if I was "The Man Who Fell to Earth" communicating to the mother ship.

When I was a kid, I used to play a random sequence of notes on the piano and go into a trance. My dad would freak out and tell me to stop "banging on the piano" and get piano lessons. My sister's piano teacher came to the house to give her lessons. His name was Mr. Merriman. I heard his name as Mr. Merry-Man. He was always happy. I figured that he had to live up to his name.

Life back then was looking more and more like a great theatrical event—Mr. Merry-Man, the laughing piano teacher; The Hooker Chemical Company, responsible for polluting Love Canal. The signs were everywhere that the world was more like a dream, and the only way to wake up was to die: then we would see it was only a dream and that time and space are merely constructs of mind.

Somehow, I knew I would always be taken care of. That I was free—free to bliss out playing my trance music to the invisible ships floating above the Twin Towers at the foot of West Broadway. Occasionally, someone would stop and close their eyes, as if I was touching their soul. To most, I was someone they just didn't get. To them, like my dad, I was just "banging on the keyboard."

I began to have a strong desire to make life art! For me, technology was the key to merging art into the mainstream. I looked at all possible media. And then I discovered an entirely new medium. Color Xerox. This new technology allowed me to experiment with light, color and movement in a new way by moving images while I was copying.

I began to cut up images from 1950s and 1960s magazines and cut up headlines. I was really into cutting things up and was inspired by William Burroughs, the provocative author. Burroughs was a big influence on the punk scene and was a guest in one of my School Of Visual Arts classes where he shared about his cut up techniques. One of my favorite recording artists, Brian Eno, also worked with the notion of cut ups. When I heard his album *Another Green World* in 1974, I was reminded of the reason I collected records. And Eno was living in my neighborhood and producing local artists for an album called *No New York*.

Being intoxicated by making art is a great joy. I randomly selected pictures from my cut up images and would swirl them around on the glass top of the copier as it was copying. I lived for the copy shop on Broome Street. And then, I won a contest in SoHo. I had free access to a color Xerox machine for an entire week. I began to create Xerox books. I began to sell them at the art bookstore in Tribeca called Printed Matter, and one of my pieces was part of a traveling show called *Electrographic Art*. To live in SoHo during the late seventies was truly what I had dreamt of, and eventually the artists I had dreamt of meeting were all around me too.

One day in 1978, one of my all-time artist dreams came true: I got to show my work to Andy Warhol. Although I was fascinated with his work, he lived up to his reputation as being pretty detached, cool and he left me scratching my head. He told me my art "would make great wallpaper." At first it felt like an insult but eventually I understood what he meant.

The Nonson Gallery a few blocks away from my home was producing the first Punk Art Show. I put one of my Xerox on plexiglas pieces in the group show along with other artists including Joey Ramone who dipped a toothbrush in red paint and hung it from the ceiling and called it *Bloody Toothbrush*. To me the punk scene was very superficial and nihilistic. Yet I saw an interesting culture of artists exploring the boundaries of art and life, noise and music in performance spaces in raw lofts. I began performing, tangling myself in wires and electrical effects.

As a graduate of the School Of Visual Arts, I went to the video studio to see if I could find a student to help me produce a video for a performance. I met a shy curly-haired guy named Keith Haring who was open to being my cameraperson and co-creator. We covered the walls of the SVA television studio with black-and-white Xerox copies of newspaper headlines and photos and then proceeded to rip them down like I was ripping wallpaper off of a wall. Then I began smashing record albums like an insane person. Keith was looking to get his work shown in SoHo and I got him into a group show at the Nonson Gallery. Keith had a special way of drawing—as the world would soon discover.

As I combed the used bookstores for images to cut up, under a stack of *Boys Life* and *Tiger Beat* magazines, was a pile of UFO magazines. I began to cut and paste pictures of UFOs into my color Xerox collages. I became obsessed with the UFO as an icon. I knew they were coming back. They were we in the future. The movie *Close Encounters of the Third Kind* had just opened in theaters, and this was the clue. I knew that the time was at hand when they would disclose we are not alone. Jimmy Carter saw a UFO in Georgia. Even Ronald Reagan, as governor of California, had seen one.

I felt like an emissary, a self-appointed goodwill ambassador—like these were my friends, and somehow I had something to do with them. They were positive, higher evolutionary beings. They were not to be feared but rather welcomed. I was them in the future, and I had come from the future to save the past. That was my emerging personal mythology.

In 1979, I had a show called *Extraterrestrial Communications* at the Nonson Gallery on Wooster Street in SoHo. It was my mission to bring the message that we are being prepared for a space-time overlap with these higher evolutionary beings. Here I saw the revolution in front of me. The ships were out there somewhere beyond visibility. They were in our heads: symbols of salvation, a return to a more whole state.

And then one day during my show in SoHo, something magical happened. I was sitting on a stoop on West Broadway when a white limo pulled up. John Lennon and Yoko Ono jumped out. The master art revolutionaries! There they were, gallery hopping! I followed them down to the corner of Prince and Wooster Streets. They slipped into a gallery across the street from the Nonson Gallery. I waited inside the Nonson Gallery, where my work hung, hoping they would cross the street and I would be able to greet them.

I had a paranoia that people thought I was crazy because I was obsessed with UFOs and drawing extraterrestrials that looked similar to my childhood imaginary friend Green Boy. Maybe John and Yoko would validate me by understanding my *Extraterrestrial Communications* artwork. Instead, they were whisked away in their limo. First and last time I saw my childhood idol.

Years later, I was listening to a song by John Lennon on an album of outtakes. The song, *Nobody Told Me*, includes the lyric, "There's a UFO over New York, and I ain't too surprised." Turns out in 1974 John Lennon stepped out on the balcony of his New York apartment and saw a saucer-shaped ship hovering close by.

Hall Of Mirrors

It was time to get grounded! I got a below-ground-level position in the mailroom of the Museum of Modern Art. Literally in the basement! It wasn't long before I injured my foot and they needed to elevate me to above the ground. I became the courier to the curators, the people who determined art history—and I was picking up their dry cleaning. But still I would dream. I dreamt that I would be part of a new art movement—a form of expressionistic revolutionary pop with a mystical twist. I imagined what this movement would be called in art history books.

On Wednesdays, when the museum was closed, my museum-guard friends would let me hang out on the gallery floor and chill by the art. I was especially obsessed with Vincent Van Gogh's drawing of the corridor in the mental hospital in Arles. I felt I knew this place and time, and I wondered if I was Van Gogh in a past life. I could actually smell the smell in the hallway. Hear the sounds. I sensed that I could have a direct connection to Vincent through his drawings. I felt his pain, his intensity.

My myth of being the starving and insanely passionate artist did not mix with being the errand boy to a couple of elitist curators who were amused by my attire. I felt like a traitor to my revolutionary-artist identity. My mirrors were everywhere, always reminding me that if I did not live my true authentic life as an eccentric radicalized artist, I would shrivel up and die.

And then one day I was in the subway and saw a white drawing on a black poster of a spaceship radiating a baby. It was Keith Haring drawing mystical political and apocalyptical hieroglyphics in the subway. Had he seen the spaceships as well? The signs were everywhere. The art revolution was in full throttle!

I.J. ROSEN

I quit my job at the museum and worked selling Warhol prints in a commercial art gallery on 6th Avenue down the block from the Waverly Theatre. I worked until midnight and always had to walk past the throngs of costumed youth waiting to the see and sing along to the midnight showing of *The Rocky Horror Picture Show*. Live.

I lived on vegetable stir-fry and falafels from Bleeker Street in my prewar flat near Prince Street. With no sink in the bathroom, I washed my dishes and paintbrushes and brushed my teeth in the same sink. My parents could not stand visiting me. They couldn't understand why I did not just go to work with my dad selling lighting fixtures rather than living in the neighborhoods their parents had come to after passing through Ellis Island.

One day I was playing my battery-operated synthesizer on West Broadway and this guy named Richard invited me to his loft to record with him. He had a Mini-Moog and a TEAC portable studio and we named ourselves The Quantum Slicing Machine. I wrote songs like *Atomic Chemistry Set* and *I was Crawling On The Floor And It Tore*. All of the existential angst of my gravitationally-trapped existence burst out with force.

I hung with Al Diaz and joined a band he was creating called Elephant Dance. I played my Electro-Harmonix touchpad synthesizer through an analog delay and accented the percussion-heavy band with cosmic noise. We played a couple of gigs around the Lower East Side and my favorite haunt was Tier 3. Tier 3 was the club down the street from the immortalized Mudd Club—but Tier 3 was the real deal. There were so many musicians in the band we could hardly fit on stage. Al was a great percussionist and the other half of SAMO—the famous downtown intelligent graffiti art duo along with Jean-Michel Basquiat.

I first met Jean-Michel when he sold his postcards and T-shirts in front of the Museum Of Modern Art. I did not know if he was a homeless person but he seemed to embody the crazy-eyed artist revolutionary, I so identified with. I invited Jean-Michel into the group show at the Nonson Gallery and the owner George Staples wanted him in the show too. But the next morning Jean-Michel tagged the gallery window with a SAMO quote and was blacklisted. Jean-Michel went on to become one of the most influential artists of his time and has left his mark on art history. He left this world too soon.

When I got fired from my job selling Warhol prints, I became more isolated. I haunted the used electronic parts stores on Canal Street collecting brightly colored transistors and other electronic parts and embedded them into my paintings that I had created on plexiglass. I was a self-fulfilling prophecy. I was an enigma. I was losing myself in my art. I was becoming art. I was in a mad search to discover the interior and exterior dimensions of the universe. My paintings and collages incorporated spaceships and DNA: they told a mystical apocalyptic story. But I wanted to get to higher states.

And then I met Robert. He was a reincarnated wizard who had a penchant for mushrooms and music. We played music together and he turned me on to magic mushrooms. Robert had seen my paintings of Green Boy and told me that he had seen the same being when he took mushrooms on a beach in Jamaica. He hooked me up with a big bag of mushrooms that eventually ended up in my meals—from stir-fry's to mushroom-spinach-cheese omelets. I came to understand that these mushrooms were put on the planet to help us communicate with nature.

In New York City, nature is very human—canyons are made of glass and steel and the most dangerous animals move in shiny metal boxes. One night I had eaten my fair share of mushrooms and was wandering through the streets of the East Village. Out of nowhere, two young men cornered me. One had a gun and pointed it at my chest. Instantly, I popped out of my mushroom trip and looked straight into the eyes of the kid with the gun—I could actually feel that he would have no remorse wasting me right there.

Then, I felt like time stopped—like I could rearrange the dream. I reached into my wallet and pulled out five one-dollar bills. I continued to make direct eye contact with the guy with the gun. We were in a moment of no time and no space. We were in the void! This was my first recollection of what I call my zero-point experience. Time stood still, as if I could rearrange reality. I waved the five one-dollar bills. The one without the gun grabbed them, and I ran without looking back. I had messed with time and space and learned how to walk in and out of reality—or was it the mushrooms showing me the rubbery nature of reality?

Life was getting dangerous wandering the streets of Lower Manhattan in the wee hours tripping my brains out. I began to discover a gaping hole somewhere between my personality and my soul, and I began to see myself as a product of an art movement devoted to the deconstruction of everything I formally identified as self. This led me to believe that the art world was a space to kill one's ego. I wanted out before I self-destructed. I was too insecure to kill my ego.

My turning point came on New Year's Eve in 1979. It was just before midnight when the mushrooms began to take full effect. I was wearing my metallic silver spray-painted London Fog and paint splattered clothes. It was a cold night and there were throngs of people wanting to get into the Mudd Club. It was an elitist scene. Limos brought the jet set down to the bowels of Lower Manhattan to rub shoulders with the trashy punk artists and other postmodern mutants. Opposites attract. Rich people digging trashy cool art types making them feel young and hip—glamorizing poverty and glorifying darkness and pain.

Because I clearly was a local artist and weird enough, I passed the code to walk through the mob of punky young suburbanites freezing their leather-skirted asses off.

On the first floor of the Mudd Club, people seemed to have fun mostly dancing their frozen toes off. As for the top floor, you had to be special or really weird to be admitted.

Because I officially qualified as weird I was led up to the top floor where all the beautiful people were. Warhol, models and rock stars. All cool! The coolest people! And suddenly I felt this icy place in my chest begin to melt. Everyone appeared to be wax sculptures posing for the camera. I needed to leave the club fast. I had eaten way too many mushrooms. Nothing seemed real anymore. I did not seem real anymore. I felt like the whole place was going to explode. I needed to get out of there. The feeling of being gravitationally trapped Light took me over.

I pushed my way down the stairs against throngs of wildly dressed punks dying to see the coolest people on the top floor. I bolted out the door and through the crowd of those still desperately waiting to get in from out of the cold. I began to run through Lower Manhattan feeling like I was melting from the inside. Melting away the frozen place inside of me. And then I had a vision. I looked behind me at the towering World Trade Center buildings and I saw both towers crumble to dust. I ran harder and harder. I needed to find another way. It was 1980. I stopped eating mushrooms. I stopped eating meat.

Self-Erasure

I began to radically change my lifestyle, starting with the purchase of a guidebook to yoga. In 1980, yoga was not a contemporary commodity or a billion dollar industry as it is today. It still had an esoteric aura to it. I practiced every position in the book on my living room floor. My favorite position was the plow. I would lie on my back, lift my legs and then extend them over and behind my head until my feet touched the floor. I loved to feel the stretch at the base of my spine.

One day, I relaxed into the plow and began to feel my body enter a paralysis. With a sudden burst, I felt as if something ripped from my trunk all the way up through my spine. It sounded like the ripping of cellophane. Within an instant, I discovered myself floating above my body. Beyond the ceiling, I seemed to enter a field made entirely of stars. It was as if I was in outer space and outer space was in me. The sound was a deep OM-like tone beyond anything I could hear in the audible spectrum or can even begin to describe now. Was it what Pythagoras called the music of the spheres or what the Ancients called *nadi*, "the sound current?" The sound was coming from within. I was the sound.

Being seamlessly merged with the Light and sound gave me comfort I had never felt in the material world. I knew I was perfect, exactly as I was. And at the same time, I did not really exist, because I was existence. I understood beyond any thinking that space, time and matter are simply phenomena pulsating out of this state of pure being.

That the universe: infinite consciousness, infinite intelligence is who I truly was!

And, this Divine Creator was within every particle of Creation. Creator and Creation were not separate. I finally felt like I was home!

People who have near-death experiences say that they see their whole life pass before them. I had such multidimensional awareness that I could see my life—past and future as projections from the still center of the present. I was the Creator. I was the void. Everything existing in nothing!

And then I slipped into the gap. I completely disappeared, and all of the impressions vanished from my conscious memory. I had what a Zen monk called "self-erasure." And I blew my fucking mind! As soon as I felt fear, within an instant, I felt the formlessness dissolve and experienced a sense of descending that

I can only describe as what the feeling must be like if thrown out of an airplane at 25,000 feet without a parachute.

Before I knew it, I was lying on the floor, flat on my back, not knowing how I got out of the plow position. Gravity felt overwhelming. I discovered I was fully paralyzed and could not even lift my arm off the ground, as if I was pinned to the floor.

Looking up at the four walls was one of the most frightening experiences of my life. The square shape of the room made me feel trapped in a box. I felt like I was, literally, in a very large coffin filled with furniture. The vibrating buzz in my skeleton and muscles persisted for at least twenty minutes and reminded me of the time I stuck a hairpin in an electrical socket. Eventually, I was able to peel myself off the floor and regain control over my body. Everything seemed so different, so intensely dense. For days following I walked the streets of New York City looking out of new eyes. I saw how everything and everyone was one integrated whole. Even a ride on the subway was a spiritual experience.

After much research in the local metaphysical bookstore, I discovered that I had experienced what Eastern teachers called a Kundalini experience. Kundalini is the psycho-electrical energy that runs up the spine when ignited Shakti from the root chakra meets Shiva in the crown and all charkas blast open. The consequences of a premature Kundalini opening without guidance from a guru could lead to insanity. Since my primary role model in life was Vincent Van Gogh, I figured I might be saved from insanity and instead be written off as one of those weird artist types living in SoHo.

Eating Light

Out of all the yogic teachers, I found a teacher named David, a gentle Jewish businessman raised on the Upper East Side. David taught a form of Kundalini meditation he learned from his teacher, Swami Rudrananda. I soon found out that Rudi, as they called him, was also raised in New York, was an art dealer, and had died in a plane crash. Twice a week, we sat in David's loft in SoHo, which he opened for meditation. David transmitted the Shakti through eye-to-eye contact. Sometimes, the Light would get so strong my eyes would stream tears like a river. Behind David hung large photographs of Rudi and Nityananda, Rudi's guru who lived in India and was known as a saint.

At first it felt weird, staring into this Jewish businessman's eyes, with pictures of dead swamis hanging on the wall behind him. But eventually I learned to let everything drop and discovered that the pictures themselves were radiating Light. Light was everywhere. I literally saw the track lights in his loft flicker when I got a surge of Kundalini up my spine.

No drugs, no electrical socket. This was the pure thing. Pure spiritual electricity! We meditated and we had Kriyas. Kriyas are spontaneous movements of the body. It looks like someone is getting a sudden shock of electricity. The small roomful of meditators in David's loft looked like human popcorn as many of them shook, rolled their heads and let out sounds that might make you think that someone was being shot with a Taser.

The art world was slipping away as I began to discover other worlds. I frequented the local sensory deprivation tanks and did Kundalini breathing in dark wet silence to try so hard to return to the stars and the sound current. Sometimes, when I went to bed, I would hear the sound current, the universal OM. I wondered if this was the sound of spirit flowing through life.

I drummed with my dumbec, a goblet drum, in Sufi groups. I became macrobiotic. I counted my chews. My mother questioned why I was a "microbiotic" and why I did not eat real food. I questioned what real food was. She called tofu "toad food," and she was not joking—she really thought that was what it was. My mom and dad had retired and moved to Florida. I was facing the fact that they were aging and that I had disappointed them by not taking up my father's business of selling lighting. Instead, I was trying to sell Light!

I started to feel the need to help others. I began to visit a couple of elderly people in my neighborhood. I visited an eighty-eight-year-old woman who had lived in Greenwich Village in the same apartment since the 1920s. She had met many of the great artists and writers of the times. She was blind and bedridden and had sores, but she told me stories ranging from the days of café society to experiences with an evil aide that she said wanted to poison her. I listened in awe. I wanted to help. I wanted to give. My heart began to open up more and more with the surging Kundalini.

I wanted to contribute more than just the ego gratification of making art. Making art and showing it seemed empty. Feeling another human being and creating a space for healing was becoming more appealing to me. Yet, I continued to make art. More abstract art. I never showed it to anyone. I began to feel like my eighty-eight-year-old friend—living as a recluse, staying away from clubs, cafes and galleries. I did not feel the need to show my work to anyone. Rather it was my inner exploration space. I created my own symbolic language. I began to write things on my paintings about ultraviolet light and DNA and other obscure concepts that seemed to come from somewhere else. I began to believe that the human species was going through a mutation, that increased ultraviolet light coming through the suspected ozone hole would mutate our DNA, and the human dimension would become more transparent. I began to think that my blood was going through a transmutation and I would soon be able to heal. I took classes in polarity therapy and read books about electromagnetic healing and psychic energy.

I also got a normal 9-to-5 job as an assistant to Joe Caroff, the graphic designer who designed the famous "007" logo. As a kid, I drew this logo on my notebooks and my homework assignments.

Joe also designed the *West Side Story* poster. As a child, that image on the record album cover fascinated me because the movie was bigger than life, and I wanted to be a "shark." We designed the posters for Woody Allen's movies. Joe's office was in the Brill Building in the center of Times Square.

I rode my bike uptown to work every day. In my backpack was a kalimba, also known as a thumb piano. During the summer, after work, I would ride my bike to Central Park and play the kalimba with chopsticks before doing yoga barefoot on the Great Lawn. I was less interested in clubs and galleries and more focused on balance and harmony.

I started getting out of the city. I hitched a ride to a yoga ashram in the Catskills, and one summer I took a Greyhound bus up to Vermont to Bennington College where The Omega Institute was at the time. The following summer, they moved to Upstate New York, and I did a work-study program living at The Omega Institute's new campus in Rhinebeck. I was introduced to all sorts of great teachers, swamis, therapists and healers. I discovered how to drum people into a shamanic journey and heal the soul. I drummed with the Sufi's in the mountains of New Mexico. I was ready to travel further, deeper on my path. Things happened. Money came from out of the blue—and a letter that would take me to the other side of the world and beyond.

CHAPTER TWO: INITIATION — CHILDREN OF THE SUN

"We are the children of the sun
Our journeys just begun
There is room for everyone"
—Dead Can Dance

Shining Path

In 1984, I received an invitation from Alberto Villoldo, PhD, to travel to Peru and study with Don Eduardo, a master *curandero* also known as a shaman or medicine man. The journey was described as a shamanic initiation into the Children Of The Sun lineage. At first, I could not imagine making such a journey, but signs that I needed to go started showing up everywhere.

It all started with Shirley MacLaine. Her book, *Out on a Limb*, was just released. In it she wrote about encounters with spaceships in Peru. I wondered if this was my invitation to reconnect with my friends from the stars. I went to my local bookstore in Greenwich Village and picked up Shirley MacLaine's book. The hardcover tome was handed to me in a snug paper bag. I walked out to my car and put the bag on the passenger seat. When I arrived home, I grabbed the bag and discovered it was empty. I checked the floor and under the seat, but the book was gone.

I had a sense that the book must have dematerialized. Was I going crazy? Somehow, this Don Eduardo dude was calling me. I decided to buy a book written by an anthropologist, Douglas Sharon, about experiences with Don Eduardo. Sharon's book, *Wizard of the Four Winds*, was out of print. I first called my local Greenwich Village bookstore; but it was not in their system. I proceeded to call almost every used bookstore in New York, but still to no avail. The book was nowhere to be found.

One day, I was in the Greenwich Village bookstore where I bought the dematerialized Shirley MacLaine book. It was a cold night, and I dropped one of my gloves on the floor in the occult section. As I reached to the floor, I noticed the spine of a book on the bottom shelf which read, *Wizard of the Four Winds*. How did that book end up in the same store that did not have it in their system and told me it was out of print? Suddenly, I could feel laughter in the ethers. Someone was playing tricks with me. It was becoming clear to me that I was on my way to a life-changing experience in Peru.

It had been almost three years since I had taken mushrooms to find answers. Now, only daily meditation was on my menu. And yet, I was getting the sense that my experience with plant medicine was not over. Don Eduardo used a variety of psychoactive plants for initiatory and ceremonial purposes. I felt safe with him and knew that these experiences would be supervised.

I met the others on the trip, about a half dozen folks from the United States and Europe, in Lima at the airport. We arrived together at the elegant Grand Hotel in Lima, only to discover that the Shining Path Maoist guerrillas had blown up the water supply. Such an elegant bathroom with fancy faucets—but no water.

The material world was about to slip away as we prepared to meet Don Eduardo and travel to Trujillo to experience our first initiation into the tonal. The tonal was described to us as discovering our totem animals, yet the tonal represents everything with a name. Healing the tonal was about recovering lost parts of our soul. In contrast, the Nagual was described as the nameless and would be our final initiation.

Don Eduardo Calderon was a rotund man with lots of energy and a joyful, playful demeanor. And, he was the ultimate trickster. He and Alberto told us not to drink any alcohol, and yet they downed beers at dinner. We traveled to Don Eduardo's home in Trujillo to go through the first healing session. Don Eduardo had a large family. He had a kind of open-air restaurant on the beach where all his family members could eat. As he and his wife, Maria, prepared fresh ceviche from fresh caught sea bass, I began to feel my nervous energy rising. How could I eat raw fish? I was a vegetarian.

Guinea Pig Spine

That was only the beginning of my nervousness. We were told that before our first healing session, we were going to be diagnosed through a method involving the sacrifice of a live guinea pig. What had I gotten myself into? Alberto never told us we would have to witness animal sacrifices. I was a vegetarian. I was against it. What else did they not tell us?

As I worked out my issues about killing innocent guinea pigs, I finally surrendered and watched Don Eduardo use a live guinea pig as a diagnostic tool by rubbing the guinea pig on the first individual's body to pick up what was going on with her. It was a primitive kind of x-ray. After rubbing the guinea pig on her body, he pulled his knife and sliced the guinea pig open. He spoke in his native tongue and declared that the female guinea pig had a black dot on her ovaries, indicating there was something going on with this woman's ovaries. The woman began to weep as she explained that her doctors had discovered a cyst on her ovaries that needed to be removed. Everyone who went through the diagnostic process had something correlating to Don Eduardo's diagnoses.

Finally, it was my turn. I was a little creeped out by feeling him rub the cute critter along my spine and utterly irked when he sliced the poor helpless creature with his knife. He stated that my guinea pig's spine had cracked at the area of the heart, indicating that I was affected by black magic around my heart. How could it be? Black magic? Once I let go of my judgmental beliefs and resistance, I felt profound healing. Don Eduardo showed us the insides of our own bodies in a shocking, visceral way. But I started to wonder about what else I had not been told. Would I have gone on this journey if I knew beforehand that adorable guinea pigs would be sacrificed to show us where we needed to be healed? And why was I not told about this shamanic initiation?

Before the healing session, I shared a drawing I had made of Green Boy with Don Eduardo. He nodded his head, confirming that he knew this kind of being. All he said was, "Africa." What could that mean? I was starting to think that my fascination with beings from other worlds was a cover for my disdain for the world I was born into. And now we were preparing for our first all-night healing session. Don Eduardo prepared the mesa. The mesa was a blanket with an assortment of powerful objects, including crystals and statues of various saints. We all sat in a U-shaped circle with the mesa in the center.

The mesa acted as an inter-dimensional transmitter and receiver. At the foot of the mesa, a variety of staffs were stuck into the ground. The staffs acted like antennas. Once the mesa was activated, we could not leave the mesa without a staff. If I needed to take a pee, I held a staff with one hand and held my "staff" with the other hand. Don Eduardo began shaking his rattle and whistling a melody. The melody was hauntingly familiar. My soul knew this melody and I began to feel an ancient memory. After he called in all the saints and spirits, and blew mouthfuls of holy water on us, we were ready to meet San Pedro.

San Pedro is a hallucinogenic barrel cactus which Don Eduardo boiled down for an entire day to make his brew. We were informed that we would inhale through our nostrils a strange mixture of San Pedro cactus, *pisco* brandy, black tobacco juice and Tabu perfume—we could not drink it because we would instantly throw up. This way, you first have a painful burning feeling in your sinus cavity before the substance dripped down your throat—and then you have a moment before the mix hits your tastebuds. Vomiting is par for the course.

But before we could drink the San Pedro brew, we needed a special purification. Though this was a sacred shamanic initiation, it was starting to feel like a hazing into a college fraternity. We had to swallow another round of the god-awful concoction. But this time we were required to pour it into our nostril with one hand while standing in a ring of brush holding a sword in the other. Don Eduardo called to his wife Maria one word, *fuego*, as she threw some burning brush into the ring. I was standing in a ring of fire, flames licking me with their intense heat. And I was marching with a sword.

After much vomiting, ceviche and all, I was ready to drink a cup of San Pedro. The brew was bitter, but went down like water after drinking from seashells several doses of the tobacco-perfume mixture. The psychoactive power of the San Pedro began to take over, and I was thrust into an apocalyptic vision. Yet, I did not feel any fear because I was safe on Mother Earth: I was protected.

I was on the ground, with my face in the dirt, on the back of Mother Earth. And I saw her shake off all the evil in the world. I saw tsunamis, earthquakes and meteors: events that are actually happening as I write this book. I saw New York City flood and buildings crumble like sandcastles in the waves. I knew that the earth has the power to purify herself.

I saw that the black magic inside me was my materialistic programming, acquired from living in a world that denied the spirit and measured material gain, regardless of one's means to the end—a culture that lied through its teeth to manipulate people into wars for oil and degraded the earth to exploit its resources in ways that placed it on a collision course with extinction. I was woven into its fabric with my credit cards and credit scores. I was asleep as to the consequences others paid for the lifestyle I felt entitled to.

Nazca Dog / Needle and Thread

After the initial healing session in Trujillo, we traveled with Don Eduardo to the Nazca Desert. Nazca first came to my attention many years earlier when I saw pictures of the Nazca Lines. The great mystery of Nazca is centered on giant etchings on the desert floor that can only be seen from high above. The etchings are vast across the bleak desert plains and depict many animals in the animal kingdom. Also running across the desert floor are long wide lines that look like airplane runways. Some have speculated that the Nazca Lines were created by ancient astronauts or created by the pre-Incan natives to communicate with their gods in the sky.

We arrived in Nazca, took a small propeller plane, and flew over the lines. The vast animal figures seemed like information about our planet for those viewing from the sky. And there, on the side of the hill, was an etching of a small being that was known as "The Owlman," but what some refer to as "The Ancient Astronaut." The etchings seeped into my subconscious mind. It felt so familiar.

After the plane landed, we checked into the hacienda. The Shining Path Maoist guerrillas had struck in the area so soldiers were guarding the hacienda. The soldiers were sitting around the pool on the chaise lounges, automatic weapons by their sides. I was tired from the journey and took a rest. I fell asleep and had a dream. I dreamt I could fly and that I was flying over the Nazca Lines. As I was crossing over the lines in the shape of a dog, I suddenly awakened to the sound of barking dogs.

That night, we prepared for our second healing journey. Don Eduardo was cooking the San Pedro in a big tin vat. Once the sun had set, we headed out on the Nazca plains. Our second healing session was to be an all-night journey held at one of the lines called "The Needle and Thread." Don Eduardo set his mesa up at the base of a spiral. The spiral represented the spool of the thread, or coiled serpent Kundalini. The needle represented the spine and was a line as long as a football field with the thread zigzagging seven times, representing the seven chakras.

When night fell and the mesa was activated through prayer and song, we began the dreadful process of taking in the mixture of black tobacco juice, Tabu perfume, *pisco* brandy and San Pedro brew by pouring the mixture into our nostrils. This time, I lost it all. I fell to the ground. The earth was alive. The earth was sexual. And I had now transformed into a black panther. And I could fly.

As the flying black panther, I flew north and landed in my parents' home. They were sleeping as I prowled through their house smelling them—knowing that they were asleep to the spirit world. Then, I found myself flying over the suburban landscape and into a shopping mall. Nobody could see me: I was an invisible black panther prowling through a shopping mall. In the mall was a store that sold crystals, dream catchers and other healing tools.

In 1984, there were no stores—that I had seen—in shopping malls selling crystals and New Age gifts. Those kinds of stores were found only in places like Greenwich Village or Berkeley.

Instantly, I knew I was in the future and had a sense that the New Age was arriving right on time. Years later, I was in a shopping mall and saw a shop selling crystals, dream catchers and other New Age items. I began to understand that I was a visionary. These visions of the future, such as the one of the World Trade Center crumbling twenty-one years before it actually happened, were possible because the past and future exist in the present.

It was the middle of the night and time for more San Pedro. Don Eduardo took a swig of Florida Water and blew it on me. Florida Water is a cologne used for purification rites. All perfumed up and swigging the San Pedro, I was ready to venture out onto the needle to walk through the seven zigzags, to the edge of the needle, to the crown chakra. I needed to take a staff to be connected to the mesa. I selected a finely carved wooden one. As I held the staff in my hand, I saw that I had picked a staff with a dog carving at the top.

For me, this was an instant confirmation that my dream earlier in the day, in which I was flying over the Nazca dog etching, was an actual projection, and the dog was showing me the way—my seeing-eye dog for the journey into the void. I felt the staff starting to sort of pull me as if I had hold of a determined greyhound dog ready to run. As I walked out to the tip of the needle, I was a football field's distance away from the group. I realized that the staff was my only connection to them and the mesa.

Suddenly, I saw myself at the threshold of a portal. The threshold was made of giant angels; their wingspans formed a corridor, and the spreading of their wings created the waves of light that form the alphabets of matter. Wave forms. The universe consisted of waveform movements of these giant angels' wings.

It all started to come together. Space and time are mere crucibles for Life. Life is Creation. Tonal is Life. Each and every being is its own unique waveform, absorbing and radiating Life through its unique wave field. We are all our own tone, our own distinct geometry of Life. We are a one-of-a-kind crystalline structure, like unique snowflakes. And everything in existence is perfect, because the universe would not be complete without everything in existence.

Life was truly like an ocean with its countless waves. And I was a wave. The glory of Creation was astounding, and this ocean of Life was calling me to become one. Angels were joined by the devas and the elemental beings that live inside all of nature. And there in the midst of all this glory was Green Boy, calling me to put down the staff and join them in the dance of Life.

I knew if I put down the staff I would leave this world forever. Perhaps I would be discovered insane, clutching the staff, and have to be put away forever in a mental hospital. Perhaps my heart would stop and the group would discover me dead from a heart attack. I was beginning to have great fear that I was going to die on this trip. That I would exit the world via Peru!

The Spirit Canoe

Our next stop was the city of Cusco, elevation 11,000 feet. We arrived in the early afternoon and went to visit Tambomachay, an ancient sacred water purification site with three tiers of stones and three streams. I sat in silence there listening to the moving waters and my moving thoughts. I contemplated the black panther—a predator that hunts its prey by stalking it at night, dawn or dusk.

On the way back from the peaceful streams, we stopped to see the ruins in Sacsayhuamán, where thousands had died in battle with the Spaniards. I was starting to get tired and rested on a rock by a large pit. I suddenly felt nauseous and dizzy and had a vision of dead bodies filling the pit. When we arrived back at the hotel, I drank a few cups of coca tea to help alleviate the altitude sickness I was starting to feel. I was a Brooklyn boy born at sea level. And yet, I was thrilled about the next day's adventure: the train ride to Machu Picchu.

Visiting Machu Picchu was a dream I held since I first cut out a picture of it and put it on my bulletin board when I was young. This was surely one of the most special places on the planet. The train through the Andes valley of the Urubamba River is one of the great train rides of the world. The Andes people are so beautiful and colorful in their alpaca clothing and hats. Even though financially they were dirt poor, their spirits had a richness that I felt was missing in my homeland.

We boarded the train with only our daypacks; no one was sure where we were going to be that night. From train to bus, we snaked up to the top of the road into Machu Picchu, elevation "only" 8,000 feet— the views were truly heavenly. At the site, everyone in our group did their own thing. We were told to meet back at five o'clock that evening. After a fascinating and amazing day, I was hoping for a nice bed and breakfast and maybe an opportunity to take in the hot springs in the area. Nobody knew where we were going, and none of us had our sleeping bags or anything for overnight.

As the sun was setting, we had no food in our bellies. Don Eduardo and Alberto arrived, and Alberto told us he had a special surprise: they had paid off the guard to leave us alone on top of Machu Picchu for the night to do a ceremony. I was relieved that we were not going to take any San Pedro or pour perfume into our nostrils. But then I started ruminating about how cold it was going to get and that I did not have my sleeping bag. It was not long before I realized that no one was going to sleep anyway because at night you can't see the giant millipedes on the ground.

We were told we were going to do a ceremony on a special rock known as the "Death Stone," or also as the "Spirit Canoe" because it looked like a canoe with a flat area to lie on. The ceremony was about allowing the spirits to take you out of your body into the West to your place of death...to experience your death. Not since the animal sacrifice did I have such remorse about going on this journey. No one wants to see his or her own death. I wanted a warm bed and a cup of coca tea.

The night was getting colder there on top of the mountain in the middle of nowhere without even a guard on duty. Finally, it was my turn to be taken up to the Death Stone. As I lay on my back staring into the endless stars, Don Eduardo summoned my spirit to join the winds to the West and show me my place of death. I did not want to see my death. I was not ready. I resisted. I fought the feeling of leaving my body. I felt a rush of fear that this was where I was going to die, that my family would get a call from the American embassy in Peru informing them I had died of hypothermia or a heart attack on top of Machu Picchu—that they were right to have worried about me not knowing if I was going to be in a hotel. And I wasn't! When I stepped down from the Death Stone, I could see I was not in the same place as everyone else in our group. I did not complete that step in the shamanic initiation.

We never slept that night. I was beginning to feel exhausted and resistant to the journey since I could not trust what would happen next. That morning we climbed up to the peak and watched the sunrise. We then headed back to Cusco and I started to feel the altitude sickness getting to me. I felt like I was going to pass out. That night we stayed outside of Cusco and I felt like I was slipping into a coma. I needed oxygen. The hotel proprietor got me a canister of oxygen, but after thirty seconds the oxygen ran out. I could not keep myself from slipping into a state of feeling like I was on the verge of losing consciousness. I had a vision of myself hooked up to IVs. I wondered if they had all died on Machu Picchu and I had to catch up, the long painful way. I needed to be validated. I needed to persevere!

That evening, the group was going with Don Eduardo and Alberto to the sacred caves where Incan priests went to dematerialize and ascend. I decided that I could not stay behind and would go with the group, even with severe altitude sickness. I was beginning to understand that since I resisted my death experience on the Death Stone, I was going through a prolonged dying experience. We hopped into an old van and rode up a mountain as the night fell into darkness. As soon as the driver dropped us off to hike the rest of the way to the caves, the sky opened up and poured rain, soaking us to the bone. I was now somewhere between fear of catching a cold and fear of dying from oxygen deprivation.

As we were getting closer to the caves, the sound of barking dogs pierced the night. Wild dogs guard the caves. My terror overrode my altitude sickness. When we arrived at the caves, I started to feel more alert and energized. Once inside one of the caves, I was buzzing with energy and could feel all my fear lift. I had a vision of the priests going into the cave, transforming their matter into spirit, and taking their bodies with them out of this world. They understood the science of transfiguration. That night, I broke through my fear of death. I began to feel a power that wanted to enter me. The caves were a turning point and marked the completion of my tonal work.

Nagual TV Snow

After Cusco, we returned to Trujillo to complete the initiation into the Nagual. The Nagual is the nameless, no experience, and nothingness. I knew not to ask too many questions about what we were about to embark on. The Nagual initiation was performed in front of the Temple of the Moon. As we gathered in a circle, Don Eduardo pulled out a jar with a brew in it. Surprise, surprise!

The mixture we drank that night was specially made from a distilled blend of San Pedro cactus and Datura. It was a good thing I didn't have my iPhone to Google "Datura" and discover that it is poisonous and can cause delirium. Don Eduardo apparently knew what he was doing with his plants, and at this point I fundamentally trusted Don Eduardo—trickster and all.

We ingested the blend and sat in a circle halfway between the Temple of the Moon and the Temple of the Sun. One by one, Don Eduardo led the initiated to stand facing the facade of the Temple of the Moon. When each initiate returned to the circle, they appeared to have a telepathic knowingness of... something. I could tell by the look in their eyes that they all knew something.

I was the last to go. Don Eduardo walked me up to face the temple, and then he proceeded to walk towards the rock wall. As he walked right up to the wall, he began to flicker, like a strobe light was illuminating him, until he literally dissolved into the rock. He was invisible. If you ever saw the movie *Field of Dreams*, where the baseball players disappear into the cornfield, this was a similar phenomenon.

The entire temple facade became pure vibration. No longer a solid mass, it was a wall of oscillating energy. I felt as if my entire field of vision shifted to what appeared like the snow on a television set. I experienced the three-dimensional world as the entire mass of twinkling stars set in the blackness of space. Similar to my Kundalini experience, I began to remember that the world as I knew it was pretty much a dream. A projection of mind! I understood that the Nagual is nameless because it is utter nothingness. It is from the nothingness that everything appears.

The Nagual is the fundamental field out of which all matter is born, thus a context for the quantum field theory discussed by physicists or the Tao of the mystical East. The ancient Sanskrit *sutras* state that "form is emptiness and emptiness is form." Jewish mystics recognize one of the highest spiritual names, Ayn Sof, as "utter nothingness." The scientific mind has attempted to define the infinite nothingness: whether it is called the *ether*, *quantum field* or the *virtual state vacuum*, it is void of matter but filled with energy. Or it is called the *plenum*, infinitely full rather than empty.

None of that is important. All that really is important is that you can trust the void! In the void, you realize that when you add everything up, it all equals zero. You can't a-void it! It is a dream, temporarily appearing to be frozen in matter—an illusion of perception. Just as the television image is an illusion of perception. Even though you watch the tube and for the moment you are engaged, the image is only dots of light flickering on a screen.

In the Tantras of the Far East, it is said that God created Maya as an illusion by leaving to the eye an incomplete and finite image in order to hide the reality and fundamental truth of the universe. Is it possible that we are all players in God's television broadcast? Could this be the real MTV: Maya Television? Is it possible that our brain and nervous system construct a tangible reality out of a cosmic dance of consciousness? If so, the constructs of our physical reality are dreamlike, and it is the collective dream that dictates what is real and what is illusion. As the collective consciousness transforms, the outer world will transform to reflect this shift.

What I experienced in the initiation gave me a new contextual framework for reality. I was left with the understanding that what I see and what I think is real may not actually exist, and what I don't see and what I imagine is unreal may really exist. I had to live with the notion that it was my identification with the drama of the phenomenal world that kept me embedded in it.

Out of the snowy quantum field reality projected itself to match my beliefs. As Don Eduardo walked out of the dance of Light and reconstituted his body, he came to me and spoke a message in Quechua. I understood every word; I actually heard it in English. "The world as you know it is upside down. You are here to turn it right-side up. You are like a sunflower. Go back to your land and spread seeds."

CHAPTER THREE: THE SCIENCE OF TRANSFIGURATION

*"Watching the signs taking over from the fading day
Changing water into wine."*
Brian Eno—Golden Hours

Crystal Chakra Dreamtime

The year was 1984, and I arrived back from Peru with a new lease on life. I bought a blue Honda Civic hatchback that I named Earth One, packed up all my belongings, including over a hundred cassettes of recorded music and spoken words, and began my journey west to California. On my way across the country, I stopped in a small freaky town in Arizona called Sedona. In 1984, there was very little going on in Sedona. I happened upon a café called Food Amongst the Flowers, and slipped inside for a bite. A woman with intense eyes was sitting next to me, also alone. She must have been in her mid-sixties, and I wondered if she was trying to flirt with me. We struck up a conversation; she told me she was psychic and was guided to share something with me.

She said I was on an important journey that would take me through many trials and tribulations, but that my destiny was to become a tycoon and use my money for good on this planet. It was easier to digest the veggie burger I was eating than the information she imparted to me. The last image I had of myself was that of a tycoon. I just wanted to be a loving, caring human being. I wanted to serve! After she finished speaking, the woman squeezed my hand and walked out into the crisp night air.

That night, I pitched a tent in the desert and fell deep asleep. Needing to pee in the middle of the night, I unzipped the tent and looked up to a sky dripping with stars. Suddenly, I saw a green light flashing in the sky. I was transfixed. Was this my first UFO sighting or was this some kind of secret military airplane? And then, in an instant, the flashing green light darted across the sky at a faster speed than any manmade object could travel. Had I been given the green light? What was ahead for me?

The next day, I traveled to Los Angeles to visit a friend. After a couple of days there, I knew it was time for me to move on. I left my friend's house after dark to head north to San Francisco. Somehow, I turned the wrong direction and found myself in a sketchy part of town. I needed gas and figured I would stop for directions. As I walked toward the glass-enclosed gas station attendant's booth, I noticed a tall, disheveled man standing by my car.

I started to feel like I was about to be jumped, with no one around except the attendant in the booth who appeared oblivious to the outside world. The man who stood by my car looked me in the eyes and said, "Hey brother, I will pump your gas for you." Clearly, this man was not associated with the gas station. I nervously said, "That's okay, I'll do it." The man insisted. Clearly, he was going to do something—either rob me or panhandle. I was uncertain and felt frozen. Finally, I said, "Sure." He proceeded to pump the gas, which I had prepaid with cash.

After he topped off my tank and screwed the gas cap on, I prepared to give him some money, hoping that was all he wanted.

As I reached for my wallet, he softly spoke, "I do not want your money. I just saw that you were a kind person and like to do kind things." Still on my guard, I rattled off some platitude about how nice he was. He told me it was a bad area, and he wanted to make sure nobody would roll me. He began to tell me his life story filled with hardship and sadness.

He told me he was stabbed in the back and should be dead. He took his shirt off and turned around to show me his back. Covering his entire back was a tattoo of Jesus on the cross with a knife cut diagonally across the midsection of the tattooed Jesus. He said that most people who believe in Christ don't really follow his teachings to love each other. He touched me in a way I will never forget. Appearances can fool you.

I decided to travel up the coast north of San Francisco and stay with another friend. It was late, and I was tired, and my foot was heavy on the accelerator pedal as it was now the middle of the night. Out of nowhere, I saw lights behind me—blue and red. I was being pulled over. The CHP officer was a tall handsome man with big eyes; he peered into my car, illuminating his view with a flashlight.

After I showed him my license and registration, he asked me where I was going. "Marin County," I answered. "Do you know how fast you were going?" he asked. Without waiting for an answer, he continued referring to my bumper sticker," Visualize World Peace—what do you do?" I told him I am on a journey. He then gave me a look filled with compassion and said "you look like a good soul, slow down, no reason to rush" and wrote me a ticket. I genuinely thanked him as he handed it to me. It was if he was an angel giving me a message, like Juan had. I was being watched over. The green flashing light I'd seen in the desert had welcomed me to my new life.

Marin County in the 1980s was ground zero for the New Age movement. I discovered a culture marinated in mellow. I came to my first four-way stop sign in Mill Valley and did not know what to do when the people who had the right of way signaled to me to go first anyway. Wasn't anybody in a rush? Instead of clubbing, I discovered gatherings: a combination of group meditation, chanting, drumming, and sharing.

Many New Age people changed their names to reflect their inner spirit. They chose names like Oceana Ecstasy, Gaia Dancer, or Hindu names such as Dharma and Shiva. Most of the New Age people I met were involved in healing, in one way or another. Healers were healers to other healers, and they spent much of their time healing themselves and studying with the numerous teachers, swamis, shamans, and therapists that facilitated workshops on healing.

The language of New Agers focused on facilitation, transformation, immersion, initiation, and manifestation. The common phrases spoken were: creating your own reality, working the law of attraction, healing your shadow, opening up to spirit, and channeling your higher self. New Age gatherings served potluck vegetarian food. If someone brought a chicken or bottle of wine, they may have felt awkward but within a blink the empty bottle and the carcass of the chicken would be all that was left.

Pot smoking was frowned upon because it supposedly put holes in your aura. But if you smudged your joint with sage and called it sacred herb, it could be considered medicine and used in sacred moments. Just don't tell anyone you are cheating on enlightenment. Most New Age folks had altars with pictures of incarnated and disincarnated masters: Christ, Buddha, Babaji, various Eastern swamis, and Divine Mothers. Crystals were everywhere—worn around the neck, placed on the altar, even buried in the yard in geometric grids to activate the property and make sure negative energy stayed far away. But I took it further!

I scored a dozen Herkimer diamond crystals, known as dream crystals. I decided to experiment. At the time, I was reading a book on lucid dreaming and decided to affix, using surgical tape, one crystal to each of my seven chakras, directly on my naked body. The crown chakra was easy. I wore a cap with the crystal taped on the inside resting directly on my crown. Taping the other crystals to my forehead, throat, chest, and belly were a little more challenging. Crystals at the first and second chakras were slightly awkward.

The Sanskrit term *chakra*, meaning spinning vortex of energy, had become common in the West among those involved in yoga and metaphysics. Imagine these chakra centers as transformers and transducers of spiritual electricity. Each chakra connects into a major nerve plexus (interlacing of nerves) and a major gland in the endocrine system. Acting as transformers, the chakras step down the subtle energy that flows through the universe.

To me, going to bed meant being wired to higher dimensions. With my journal at my bedside, I visualized a pink lotus flower and fell asleep, only to wake up every few hours remembering my lucid dreams and writing them down in my journal. My lucid dreaming became increasingly vivid. In many of my dreams, I confronted danger and realized that I was dreaming and could control my reality. If I encountered a gang of muggers, I could tease them with my disappearing act and make them fall on their weapons. I was discovering my power and healing my past!

I had dreams of driving off a cliff and being able to fly with the car. I even discovered I could fly by breathing gently in my dream. When I began to feel fear in my dream, my breathing became heavier and I would start descending and wake up before crashing. Many nights, I woke up every couple of hours to write about my lucid dreams in my journal. When I woke in the morning, my day would seem more dreamlike than my nighttime dreams. I was starting to feel more transparent, less dense, and I became fascinated with the concept of the "Light body."

Light Body, Heavy Heart

As I read books about the Light body, consciousness, and healing, I began to understand that the body is a vast network of many different types of life energies. From the flow of oxygen to the flow of blood, these energies are continually at work recreating the You that you know to be your Self. Beyond the molecular level are subtle systems of life energy that connect us with the infinite universal energy Source. This life force that energizes living systems is called by many names. In the East, it is described as *prana, ki,* and *chi*. In the West, scientists have called it *orgone (Reich),* and *bioplasma*. In Western religion, the references to the *Holy Spirit* or the ancient Hebrew word *ruach* refer to a life force that is finer than the physical. Let's just call it "spiritual electricity."

This spiritual electricity is absorbed and flows through various energy centers and channels. There are numerous systems that offer blueprints for how the physical body utilizes this energy. The people of ancient China discovered the network of pathways known as meridians. The oriental system of acupuncture uses fine needles to stimulate the hundreds of meridian points. This helps restore the flow of life energy to parts of the body that are blocked or diseased. From the Vedic sciences of India, the teachings of a network of subtle energy pathways, called *nadis,* help expand our understanding of energetic anatomy. The *nadis* form a web of life energies composed of 72,000 or more fibers.

With all this knowledge flooding in, I still felt something missing in my life. I heard the message repeatedly from powerful women healers that I was bypassing the emotional body and could not heal until I felt my feelings. One day, I was at the local natural food store and saw a flyer for something called "Electronic Body." A woman named Fran, who was from Texas, was giving a workshop in which people hold various points on the body until they release negative emotions, pain, trauma, and psychic poisoning. I called the number on the flyer and spoke to a very gentle woman who was sponsoring the workshop at her house. After an hour-long chat with her, I was convinced that this work would help me in many ways to heal myself.

I was told that I needed to buy a certain kind of liquid trace minerals that would help to conduct the body's electrical current. I arrived at the workshop with my trace minerals and a notebook. After an introduction to the work, we split into small groups of three or four. One person would lie down and the others in the group would hold certain points. Everyone had the chance to have his or her points held. Most people did a lot of crying as their points were held and they were releasing deep emotions. One of the fellows in my group, a German man, had a particularly cathartic experience. His body flailed as he screamed, releasing past traumas.

I was starting to get uncomfortable as I saw the trace minerals being consumed and so many people expressing themselves in such a raw way. I kept feeling resistance to having my points held. Finally it was my turn. I was encouraged to take more of the bitter tasting trace minerals, and I flashed back to Peru. Why do we have to put disgusting-tasting liquids in our body to be spiritually healed?

I lay down on the massage table, and the two women in my group began holding points. One was working on my upper body and the other holding points on my feet. As their applied pressure intensified, I began to have bizarre visions that I shared with the group in real time: one was a cigar-chomping Archangel, laughing and shouting out with a Brooklyn accent, "Training wheels! This is nothing but training wheels!" The two women holding points kept repeating, "Focus on your feelings." I could not feel anything but the pressure of the points being held, and I continued to see strange visions that made me laugh hysterically.

Fran the women teaching the workshop, came over and authoritatively told me to "get out of your head" and "start feeling." How many times had I heard the words, "get out of your head," from women healers? Finally, the German fellow joined in the point holding by using his elbow on my solar plexus. This started to make me feel uncomfortable. For some reason, I did not like this chap. Then Fran became almost abusive, telling me I was playing games and resisting my emotions. That started to get me pissed off. I suddenly had a flashback that the German man was an SS officer and he was trying to hurt me, to destroy my will, so I had to fight back.

My body started gyrating, and I began to flail as several other students joined in on the point holding. The whole room was now focused on me as I was cursing the German fellow: "You fucking Nazi pig! You mother-fucking torturer! Fuck you, mother fucker!" Fran was getting excited now—I was feeling my feelings. Actually, I was starting to feel violent toward the people in this group and I began to feel unsafe. I ripped myself from the table and darted out of the room onto the street and kept walking. When I returned, everyone suddenly cared about me, and I ended up sharing my gratitude for how they helped me to get in touch with my feelings. But inside, I was feeling that this was no way to heal.

Adam

In Marin County in the early 80s, there was a new buzz in the New Age circles. His name was Adam. He was not a person but rather a chemical compound. At that point in history, this drug—MDMA, called Adam and now known as Ecstasy or Molly—was not illegal and was being administered mostly by a small group of psychotherapists. I was told, "it opens your heart chakra and helps you feel." I was also told it was "like ten years of psychotherapy in a four-hour trip."

One day, I was in Southern California and my friend Susan told me she wanted to take me on "a journey." I wasn't sure what she meant until she pulled out a small white capsule and said, "Adam." She advised me not to eat the night before and we would do it the next morning. The next morning, we began the day with meditation and prayer to prepare for the journey. We each had a gallon of water to drink; my friend told me I needed to keep hydrated. We took the pill and within half an hour I began to feel a tingly sensation in my body and a deeper pattern in my breathing. My jaw became very tight, and I looked like I had TMJ.

Abruptly, I felt like I was hit with a truth serum. I began to express how lonely I had been in my life. Susan proposed we go out in nature and connect with Mother Earth. As I was lacing up my shoes, she suggested that we walk barefoot. There we were, crossing the Pacific Coast Highway—barefoot. Susan intentionally walked over some crushed pieces of glass in the road. The glass looked beautiful, glistening in the sun. I followed her and gently rested my feet on the glass. Everything was beautiful, including the cars zooming by. It was all so very alive! I was breathing deeply, transfixed by the beauty of the broken glass.

When we made our way into the nearby nature preserve, Susan and I became intoxicated smelling the wild mustard flowers and tasting the wild fennel. Everything was more beautiful, and I realized that I could feel very deeply. My heart was open! Maybe this was all it took. In this moment, I knew that everything was held tighter by love and that I no longer needed to live in fear. We got back to the house and I began to crash. As I was coming down, Susan took me in her arms and rocked me like a baby. I felt a deep sadness inside me. I had spent so much of my life alone. I felt I never really had a relationship worth writing about because I was fearful of being rejected. Therefore, I had rejected many opportunities to grow deep in love with someone.

The next time I saw Susan, she was getting married in a small cottage in the middle of a forest. Susan was smiling, as Sasha, my new girlfriend, and I came to share breakfast with an intimate wedding party of twelve. They had a surprise for us: Adam. The wedding party was going to be an Ecstasy party—no wonder there weren't any relatives of the bride and groom attending.

Sasha had mixed feelings, and I did too. I felt that my prior experience taking Ecstasy revealed to me the frequency I could naturally tap into by merely breathing, and I questioned whether we needed to take a chemical to access that state. My girlfriend's curiosity outweighed her fear, and we found ourselves swallowing the pills together. Peer pressure? The second time is never as good as the first, especially when the person you do it with starts freaking out. Sasha opened up and shared with me that her uncle had sexually abused her when she was twelve years old. We shed tears, I held her, and she seemed to be in a healing space.

The wedding began. The cottage smelled of an abundance of flowers and burning sage. The bride and groom were dressed in white flowing clothes and wore flowers in their hair. Someone played Tibetan singing bowls. Katherine, the only one who did not take Ecstasy, officiated the wedding. Katherine was a powerful healer and never took drugs. She said she was naturally on Ecstasy by just breathing. I could relate, but I was tempted to try it again, this time with someone I was dating.

The vows went on forever as legions of angel's names were invoked. Everyone was in a state of bliss—except Sasha. She looked sick. Just as Susan and her groom were about to light each other's candle, Sasha ran to the bathroom which was only a short distance from the altar in the tiny cabin. I followed Sasha into the bathroom. Everyone was oblivious to what was going on with Sasha.

Once in the bathroom, Sasha disclosed that she was feeling terror. I informed her that terror is the reverse polarity of joy.

I whispered to her so as not to disturb the wedding ceremony just several feet from the bathroom: "Reverse the polarity." Sasha blurted out, "I can't reverse the fucking polarity!" She was kneeling by the toilet dry heaving. The entire wedding party halted as Katherine wondered aloud with grave concern what was going on. Susan's marriage did not last long. Sasha and I lasted even less.

Keys To Transfiguration

By the summer of 1985, I was living at Muir Beach on the magnificent Marin County coastline, close to the hiking trails into Muir Woods. I became a true nature lover. I enrolled in a master's degree program in art therapy and was writing a thesis on shamanism, symbols, and consciousness. I was also doing an internship at a residential treatment center for the mentally ill in San Rafael. I was now on a path of serving others, assisting them in discovering their own spiritual truth.

One of my advisors was an art therapist by the name of Mindy. Mindy took me through my own art therapy process. In my process, I began to unfold a series of symbols made from flame-like images as well as notes about DNA and transfiguration. Mindy could not quite understand where all this was coming from until one day when she saw a book at a friend's house. Upon opening the book, she saw images and words that seemed to mirror what was coming out in my art therapy. She was blown away, and she told me I needed to buy the book right away.

The book was *The Book of Knowledge: The Keys of Enoch* by J.J. Hurtak. The keys were sixty-four spiritual scientific codes about the transfiguration of the human species into the next level of evolution. I opened the book and read these words:

> "The physical form of life passed into greater 'light' and the matter-energy bodies of the faithful were advanced into fifth-dimensional bodies of Light, into the greater universe.

Hence, through a fifth-dimensional reality of Light, the physical form passed into a tremendous effulgence of Light so that they who went on as a family of faith never knew that they had 'died' in the temporality of the body." (Key 319:143)

As I read passages in *The Keys of Enoch* about increased ultraviolet light's effect on DNA, I reflected on the painting I had created in New York after my Kundalini experience in which I referenced DNA and ultraviolet light. How did I have all this information inside me? And what was the purpose for knowing all of this?

My hunger for knowledge accelerated as I began to research more esoteric information. I also continued to delve deeper into my own psyche. I found myself even more isolated, spending much time alone in nature, reading and meditating. I wanted to know where all this knowledge was coming from as I was beginning to put pieces together. I began to probe deeper into discovering the nature of my soul. I found myself in hot tubs being facilitated through rebirthing sessions. I wanted to explore my past lives but kept hitting a wall, as if I was not supposed to access that knowledge. Then, in one of my rebirthing sessions, I had a profound understanding that I had incarnated from the future to help the earth through this transition. I saw myself in what looked like an enormous space ship. The walls were made of a white crystalline structure, and I was sitting at a large round table made of the same substance.

The other beings sitting around the table seemed very familiar and profoundly intelligent and advanced, but they looked like humans. One of the beings was an older man who was the spitting image of Colonel Sanders. They told me about my mission: I was supposed to help the earth transition by producing media that would prepare people to handle the transfiguration of the physical dimension as we know it to a more transparent structure of physical reality. Even the colonel seemed to glow from the inside.

In an odd series of events, where truth is really stranger than fiction I serendipitously befriended Colonel Sander's daughter, Margaret. She was in her 80s at the time. She invited me to her home in West Palm Beach and she ordered in KFC. Margaret had a rich metaphysical orientation and told me some pretty far out things. I felt comfortable sharing some of my metaphysical experiences and I proceeded to tell Margaret that I believed I was on a spaceship with her dad in the future. And she smiled. Not as if I was crazy, but as if she knew something I did not know.

Margaret passed away in 2001. Years later, I was reading the newspaper and learned that KFC created an astronomical 87,500 square foot image of Colonel Sanders— the KFC logo— in Nevada's Area 51 desert site. It can be seen from outer space. Once again, reality as we know it appears more like a strange dream.

Though I broke my vegan diet to share a bucket of KFC at Margaret Sander's home, my interest in food was waning as I began to wonder if I could live on blue-green algae (cyanobacteria), purified water, and fruit. I also spent much of my time breathing Light into my body, believing I could metabolize Light directly as I must have done in my future life on the spaceship. After all, cows eat the grass that eats the Light. Could I photosynthesize myself? Could I receive sustenance directly from Light?

Therese Neuman, of Germany, was a woman who lived for years on a teaspoon of water a day, and was documented by a doctor who originally came to expose her as a fraud. When the great spiritual teacher, Paramahansa Yogananda passed away, his physical body was on display for 20 days without any signs of decay—this account is documented by the director of the mortuary.

I was clear that I was on a path of transfiguration and that my blood was shifting into a higher frequency, because the earth was being bathed in a new kind of Light. I believed the molecular density of matter in this dimension would make us all be more luminous.

And there was the dark side. I had fears that there were forces that did not want this New Age. There was too much destruction. I started to feel like there is an inside and an outside to creation. On the inside, everything is made of Light and is infinite and eternal. It was a domain of unity consciousness. On the outside is a world that is constantly being born and dying: a world of polarity ruled by time, space, and the belief that matter is more real than spirit.

All of the dream activation I was doing catapulted me into darker energies. I had a recurring dream that I was being given blood transfusions from evil doctors trying to abort the Divine Plan that I was here to achieve. All I could do was visualize my body being immersed in a showering of violet light, purifying the astral trails of my ego burning to dust. Somehow, I was getting way too far out. I needed to find a job. I was about to get grounded. Really grounded!

CHAPTER FOUR: CABIN IN ELK

*"I got cabin fever,
It's burning in my brain
I got cabin fever,
It's driving me insane."*

—The Muppets

Zero-Point Flames

As my money was running out, I needed to find some kind of work. I was completing my master's degree and wanted to get hours toward my registration as an art therapist. I combed the newspaper for all jobs, but especially jobs working with kids.

The job I finally found required me to move further up the coast to the hinterlands of Mendocino County in the dead of winter. My new job would not start for two weeks; I needed to find a place to live temporarily and discovered an old hippie commune. They rented out cabins. Since I had no money, they worked out a deal with me and gave me the cabin farthest away from the collective kitchen and shower. I had to park my car and walk about an eighth of a mile into the woods.

The cabin was simply a plywood pyramid with one window and no insulation. The draft blew through the knotholes on the platform floor. The wood stove was big enough for one log at a time; when it ran out, I would see my breath. There was only a hole in the ground outside my cabin. Peeing was not an issue but having to poop in the cold rain was not good.

Sometimes, I had to burn some of my notes to get the single-log fire going in the wood stove. I had some brown paper from a package and started stuffing it in the stove. My hand was inside the stove when some molten plastic tape dripped onto my index finger. Abruptly, I could feel my metabolism speed up as the pain instantly disappeared and I entered the state in which time stands still. I had been there before, that familiar feeling of time, space and matter momentarily becoming slippery as it did when I was held up at gunpoint in New York, I was in a moment of non-time: in the gap between the frames of time. It was as though I stepped out of time and reset the experience. When I finally had the courage to look at my finger, I was shocked. There was not even a red mark, and no pain.

This now familiar feeling of altering time and resetting reality was starting to make me feel that I was truly creating my own reality. I felt empowered. Within an hour of this second zero-point experience, as I called it, I was drafted to help a couple of guys move a wooden structure. I got a splinter in the same finger that I thought I had burned. The splinter wound became infected. My finger was now red from the infection.

Creating one's reality has a side effect. If we keep worrying and ruminating, we can attract events to confirm our limiting beliefs. In retrospect, I did not feel worthy to have this zero-point time-shifting ability. I needed to learn humility and compassion for myself.

Black River Ranch was a residential treatment center serving some of the youngest emotionally disturbed children in California, or as I liked to call them, children of emotionally disturbed parents of emotionally disturbed parents, and so on. The ranch was run by a psychiatrist who seemed to be very well-trained and dedicated to the growth and evolution of his staff, as evidenced by his frank and caviling approach, frequently dropping his unsolicited analytical perspectives on the staff. Free therapy—whether you liked it or not!

I was required to spend three straight days a week—the equivalent of a seventy-two-hour workweek, which included sleeping overnights—in the cabin with the children. In my group cabin, I was responsible for six boys between the ages of six and seven. The rest of the week, I lived in a shabby cabin that had no insulation and only a wood burning stove for heat, located about twenty minutes by car deeper into the forest and up on top of a ridge. The only other person that lived off of my dirt road was some old reclusive hippie.

Cracked Mirror

At the ranch, I was learning how to be a loving support for the boys as well as a disciplinarian. Discipline was definitely my weakness, and our director seemed to be watching me and encouraging me to be firmer with the boys. Almost all of the children on the ranch had experienced one or more severe forms of sexual, physical, psychological, and emotional abuse. For many of them, it was all of the above. One child named Donald, whom I had a special attachment to, became my sacred mirror for my own submerged shadow. I believe Donald appeared in my life to show me how I too had a buried rage inside me that was disguised by a peace-loving spiritual imposter. It's all Light!

At nighttime, Donald would relive the trauma of his tortuous sexual and physical abuse. It was my job to keep him safe. He would taunt me, running around exposing his penis and, at times, trying to trash the cabin so that I would have to restrain him physically, thus satisfying his need to be held. He was six years old, but was strong and a bit of a wild child. Donald was also a head-banger and could potentially crack his skull open if not restrained. As I held him in the restraint technique I was trained in, he was unable to move his arms and legs. He would buck his head into my chest and try his best to bite me. Unfortunately, Donald's acting out with me became addictive for him, and every night I found myself restraining him and trying to talk him down for at least an hour. Here I was, spending three straight days and nights without a break in this hellish place. Many nights, I was covered with Donald's spit or urine, wondering why I had chosen this path over working as a stockbroker or a plumber.

Donald was hell-bent on breaking me down. I became his obsession. The director would call me into his office and conduct spontaneous psychotherapy sessions with me, telling me I had unresolved issues with my mother. I could not relate to what he was saying, as I believed that I was raised by loving nurturing parents in the safety of suburbia. I was beginning to feel like I was in a weird cult. Yet, this was my job. I made so little money that I could not see a way to get out, so I figured I needed to go deeper and become a stronger more compassionate person. I knew I was there for a reason!

That winter was one of the rainiest winters in California's history. Being confined mostly indoors with off-the-wall kids was beginning to set me off-the-wall. One day, the rain stopped and the sun came out so I decided we were going to collect rocks and create a sacred Native American medicine wheel. The kids really got into this activity, bringing back the most unique rocks they could find. Donald seemed to be enjoying this adventure. As I was neatly placing the rocks in a ring, I felt a sudden blow to my head. Donald had tossed a rock in my direction—in the direction of my head. After the shock of seeing blood in my hair, I set off to chase Donald but soon decided I was done chasing him and focused on myself.

The ranch nurse patched me up, and I was sent to the director's office. He was sitting in his big chair behind his big desk and he looked at me with his big buggy eyes, magnified by his coke-bottle-thick glasses, as if I was in big trouble. Big trouble? After some brief unsolicited therapy about my submerged rage and counter-transference with Donald, we mutually determined that I was not in a healthy relationship with Donald and I most definitely was not in a healthy relationship with my own self. My time at the ranch came to an abrupt ending, synchronized with the abrupt ending of clear skies. That afternoon, the rain returned harder than ever and nearly washed out the road to my cabin in the hippie commune.

For several days, the rain fell with the power of the heavens. I ran out of firewood. I was forced to burn my book collection for warmth. I burned mostly books about spirituality and personal growth; they seemed to burn pretty smoothly. I did hold on to my copy of *Fahrenheit 451* by Ray Bradbury. My only companion was a lone mouse, although at times I wondered if he had a family of mice sharing the cabin. I began to write about the mouse and me. I felt even more vulnerable than he!

There was no question that I was smack in the middle of a classic "dark night of the soul." With no money to go anywhere and creeks swelling over their banks and washing out the roads, I was forced to sit still in my damp, dark cabin and contemplate the series of events I had endured at the ranch. Donald haunted me, as if I let him down by *not* hurting him and thereby confirming his belief that life and people are not to be trusted. So much damage done to this child at such a young age!

My heart felt broken. I could not stop ruminating on the idea that if I were pushed just one more inch by Donald I too would fulfill his sick notion that he was only worth the abuse he deserved for merely being alive. Donald had saturated my soul. Donald was a mirror of a part of me I was hiding from—a part of me that eked out in my misanthropic artist days in SoHo and was quickly cast away in my years as a spiritual sadhu.

Mendocino Meltdown

Finally the rain stopped and I worked my way into town. I needed to see a familiar face, so I picked up my mail at the local post office and chatted with the postmaster—a jovial, gossipy old woman named Blanche. Blanche knew where everybody lived and was anxious to share the biggest news in town that took place just a stone's throw away from my cabin. The old reclusive hippie I never saw had blown his brains out with a shotgun during the time I was at the ranch. He was a Vietnam veteran with a history of post-traumatic stress disorder and depression.

This news, somehow, was like the final push off my ledge of sanity. I wondered if I was next in line for making the local gossip. For some reason, the ranch director had me looking at myself as a closet homicidal maniac ready to explode at the drop of a dime. I needed help. I needed counseling from someone who could confirm or deny that I had it in me to commit violence. So I wandered into the local community counseling center. The director of the center recommended that I show up for a group therapy session—believe it or not—later that evening. After much internal debate, I figured I had nothing to lose, since I felt I had already lost my sanity.

At seven o'clock, I wandered into the meeting space and was introduced to a group of five men. Each man had been ordered by the court to participate in therapy for some sort of domestic abuse. I felt very much out of place. I was a young, wild-eyed, twenty-something New Age Light healer, into playing drums and chanting "Om," sitting in a circle of gruff worn-out married men who resembled a crew of lumberjacks. I could tell that I was more or less tolerated as opposed to being welcome into the wife-beater tribe.

The first person to share looked like a prototypical lumberjack draped in an oversized black-and-red wool shirt. His beard was full and his red lips were drastically framed by the blackness of his beard—he looked like a cartoon character. As he recapitulated the last time he attacked his wife, I began to feel a powerful energy overwhelm me in an unfamiliar way. It was different from the classic Kundalini surge I experienced before. It felt more like the tornado that spun Dorothy over the rainbow. As the lumberjack wife-beater became more animated—now resembling Popeye's arch nemesis, Bluto—and dramatized how in a fit of rage he picked up a chair and heaved it across the room toward his wife, I cracked up into a hysterical fit of laughter. I laughed uncontrollably, sobbing at the same time, and my body was trembling. If the group leader did not act as swift as he did in removing me from the room at that moment, I would have been thrown faster than the chair the lumberjack had thrown in his story.

I was left alone for several minutes, isolated in the lounge at the community health center, as the group leader cancelled the group and returned to attend to me. Those several minutes, waiting, felt like an eternity. I was ticking like the clock on the wall, uncertain as to how I would explode. When the group leader came back into the room, he informed me that he was concerned that I was in the midst of a breakdown and suggested I get some urgent counseling at the community hospital with the on-call psychologist. Not trusting what was happening inside my body, I succumbed to his suggestion.

At the hospital, my gut instinct returned to me, and I realized my visceral desire for catharsis would be better managed in a breath-therapy workshop than an involuntary admission to a psych ward. But perhaps it was too late. I crossed over the threshold and entered the world that was familiar to Donald—the world of labeling. I quickly came down from the shock of what I had done and pretended that I was all better and ready to go home to my mouse and company in my lovely drafty cabin.

The on-call psychologist was a tall Amazon of a woman who sized me up as if she could see through my veneer of "I'm okay, you're okay: let's call the whole thing off." After two hours of grueling questioning about my background, including my explorations in shamanism, the psychologist rested in a pregnant pause. She told me I was very fortunate that she was trained in transpersonal psychology; she could see that I was having a spiritual crisis and that I was not homicidal or suicidal. But, she explained, she was in a real dilemma: recently, one of her clients blew his brains out. I informed her that her client was my reclusive neighbor and that the story of his suicide affected me in a profound way. After a bit of deliberation, she agreed to release me with the stipulation that she would call me first thing in the morning.

Years later, when I was working at a residential treatment facility, I was approached by a boy about fifteen or sixteen, who looked very familiar. It was Donald. He remembered me, and with a tear in his eye he said, "I remember I was very mean to you. I apologize. I was really messed up." I shook his hand and said to him, "I am so glad you reached out to me. I have thought of you often over the years. Be well." I realized that during that entire brief encounter, I never let go of the firm handshake—as if I was telling him through body language that I respected his courage. I then walked into the men's room and cried hysterically.

CHAPTER FIVE: GALISTEO BASIN

"The crow has brought the message to the children of the sun for the return of the buffalo and for a better day to come."

Robbie Robertson—Ghost Dance

The Calling

It was warming up in Elk and I was healing. I spent most of my last month hiking through the forest, meditating, and recording a piece called "Carl's House" using my synthesizer for background sound and a rant from deep in my soul about the human condition. My experience working at the ranch and my explosive cathartic episode had opened my mind to new dimensions of possibility. I had this deep inner urge to start anew. My spirit was telling me, "Santa Fe, New Mexico."

Then, strange things started happening. I began to see cars with New Mexico license plates every time I drove on Highway 101. I got a phone bill with several calls to a number in New Mexico. No one other than myself was ever in my cabin, and I never made the calls. I called the number. It was disconnected. I was starting to worry that I really had lost my mind. But everything seemed so much clearer. Lost mind? Clearer?

I sold my synthesizer and recording equipment and had enough money to drive to Santa Fe, a place where I knew no one and had no idea how I would make money. But, I drove. I arrived in Santa Fe as the sun was setting over the Sangre de Cristo (blood of Christ) Mountains. I will always remember my first glimpse of the earthy cityscape while on the radio Phil Collins was singing, "take me home, 'cause I don't remember." My eyes filled with tears, as if I was coming home. What was it that got me to pack up my belongings and $500 dollars and go to a place where I knew no one?—with one exception.

I had the name and phone number of a brother of a woman I barely knew. I found a cool café to hang out in. I put a quarter in the payphone and called the number. One phone call, and I found myself being received by Santa Fe with open arms. Alan and his wife Tonia invited me to their home. One wonderful dinner with great conversation led to one month living for free in their adobe guesthouse. My experience in Mendocino was melting away in the hot tub with the sound of coyotes howling in the background.

It was clear that I needed a break from working in anything that could be emotionally heavy. One day, I was checking the bulletin board at the natural foods store. Back then, those bulletin boards were like the internet is today if you were looking for a place to rent, or for roommates, or even for a job. It was there I ran into someone asking me if I needed a job. They were looking for another able man to help them build an adobe house in the desert.

Without any experience in construction, I said yes and was hired as the mud man. The mud man shovels mud that is used as mortar for laying the adobe bricks. We were so far out in the desert there were no roads. We sat in the back of the truck as we were driven through mountain dirt roads, eventually making our own path between cacti and rocks.

The earth was healing me! I drank a gallon of water a day. I began eating meat again. I saw my body transform and my heart open. I found my own place to live, a one-bedroom adobe cottage up a dirt road. I met a sweet woman named Kate who lived across a dry riverbed, or arroyo. Kate loved to go walking with her dogs. She loved horses. When a storm would break, the sky opened and inches of rain fell to the ground in hours. I was not able to forge the water in my Honda and was cut off from her.

The Eagle In The Tunnel

With a burning desire to make a difference in children's lives, I began to feel I was ready to look for another job working with children again. I found a job as a social worker and therapist at a boys' ranch in the Jemez Mountains. I had my master's degree in art therapy, but I had no experience as a therapist or social worker other than the ranch in California and my internship. One meeting with the director, Fred, and he was ready to hire me. Fred was an easygoing guy, yet something was wrong with this picture. He was too eager to hire a very green candidate.

Fred showed me an old adobe building that I could set up as my expressive arts studio. That was enough for me to say yes to the job. I was excited about getting some guys to paint Native American designs on the kiva fireplace and fix it up into a cool space to hang out and heal. The twenty-five to thirty boys on the ranch were some of the toughest in the state. Many of them were orphaned. Several of the boy's fathers were in prison.

The Española Valley is breathtakingly beautiful. Driving through it, it seems like a heavenly place to live. In the 80s, it was a hotbed for the drug trade. My first day on the job, I realized I was a minority. Most of the staff was Latino, and most of the boys were Latino or Native American. The staff was comprised of some pretty tough macho guys who kept the boys loosely in check based on sheer fear. I was not so welcome at first.

One of the boys, Nick, was a short fifteen-year-old who thought of himself as a *cholo*. He wore his flannel shirt open and pants low. Nick was a little guy, but he thought he was a giant. He needed to show the other boys that he was cool by walking past me and whispering to me, "We're gonna cut you up." This time, I was not going to be intimidated. I will never forget the day Nick was being transferred. He gave me a special handshake and said, "You're a pretty cool guy." There was a tear in his eye. The boys were intense, unpredictable, and at times dangerous, but I formed some special bonds with them.

Fred enjoyed going to conferences and taking five days off at a time. I was second in command because I had a master's degree, and when Fred was away, I witnessed some near deadly circumstances and needed to make some big decisions.

I saw one kid pushed through a plate-glass window in the dining room, blood squirting all over. Another boy was discovered to have a gun and would not tell anybody where the clip was. Still another kid broke into the office by smashing the window and stole the keys to the ranch truck and medication room; he made it over the Colorado state line in the stolen ranch truck with an assortment of drugs.

As the social worker, I traveled with one boy to southern New Mexico and helped him become emancipated. I took another boy home to his uncle in Las Vegas, New Mexico, only to learn later that the uncle was actually his dad who was wanted for murder and on the lam. The local police eventually found the boy in the parking lot of a Home Depot huffing paint with his father. But through all of the drama, no one ever cut me. As luck had it, Fred was forced to lay me off since the ranch was up for sale and many of the boys were being transferred.

My last job in Santa Fe was in a small group home for mentally disabled adults. It was pretty mellow, as they were a heartfelt bunch. This was an overnight position once again like in California. One of the residents was an obese man in his twenties named Ian. Ian had a disease called Prader-Willi syndrome, a complex genetic disorder in which the constant craving to eat can cause those afflicted to eat themselves to death.

Ian was a sweet friendly guy, but he needed to be constantly monitored. All cabinets containing food and the refrigerator needed to be locked at all times. One night, we were serving meatloaf for dinner. Ian was limited to one second helping. He asked for more, yet I knew he had his second helping already. Ian debated me and began to pout and whine. He stood up and reached for the meatloaf. I was quicker and removed it and began to walk back into the kitchen.

Ian was pissed and determined to get the plate of meatloaf. I panicked and dropped the meatloaf in the sink with the dirty dishes. As the meatloaf sank into the suds, Ian's hands reached into the sink, rescuing the now sudsy meatloaf, and he began shoving it into his mouth. I tried to block the 300-pound man. Then, I felt Ian's hands go for my neck. And I began to slip onto the floor. Suddenly, I found myself speeding through a tunnel, and all I can remember was seeing the head of an eagle. I heard the words over and over again, "Ian, you are going to kill him." When I was helped up from the floor, I realized I had been out of my body.

The experience shook me up. I decided to take some time for myself and discover what my true calling was. I drove north to Taos. On my way, I decided I was going to swim in Eagle Lake. Looking for a good place to access the lake, I drove down a dirt road that came to a dead end. I got out of the car to see if there was a path down to the lake. As I walked down the path, I noticed a large feather. I figured it was a turkey vulture feather and stuck it on my rearview mirror.

In Taos, I hooked up with my friend Lionel and his friend Geronimo who lived on the Taos Pueblo. We planned to go to a sweat lodge together. Lionel grabbed some firewood and blankets, and we filled the back of my car. He noticed the feather on my rearview mirror and identified it as an eagle feather. This was a big deal for me, knowing how sacred eagle feathers are. I brought the feather to the sweat lodge and prayed for a new vision for my life. My relationship with Kate had begun to fall apart and Santa Fe was feeling like my past life. I saw myself at a crossroads. I was going to go deeper into nature and live in the mountains and off the land, or I was going to move to Los Angeles and bring my spiritual vision to the entertainment world.

My quest for spiritual vision took me deeper into the wilderness. I hiked several miles up the Gila River to spend some time alone and enjoy a natural hot spring alongside the river. I had to forge the river a couple of times. I decided to scale the sandstone cliffs instead of trying to cross the river at a spot where the river was too deep to forge. As I was crossing the cliff, the ledge began to crumble. I lost my footing, as well as my water bottle, which fell away as I hung on by my hands. I regained my footing, and when I arrived at the hot springs, the sun was setting and the sandstone canyon began to glow orange. I spent most of the night in the hot spring listening to the sound of the rushing river and gazing at the path of stars shining down into the canyon. I was at peace.

The next day, I was ready to head back. When I reached the spot where I had the choice of scaling the sandstone cliffs or forging the river, I was certain that forging the river was the only way to go. It was a beautiful spring day, but what I did not realize was that the spring melt had swelled the river to such a degree that crossing it would be nearly impossible. The river was running fast and hard. I was truly between a rock and hard place. Was this how it was going to end? It was time for me to pray. I closed my eyes and saw the eagle circling inside of the tunnel. I needed to be focused, trusting, and fearless. I still don't know how I crossed the river. The water was chest high and my backpack was heavy. The river flowed with great velocity. I made it across. I still don't know how or why I was not carried downstream, backpack and all.

Harmonic Convergence

The New Age had erupted. The media began to portray it as a kooky movement led by people like Shirley MacLaine, who had recently bought property in Santa Fe. Santa Fe in the mid-80s was a New Age Mecca. I was getting sick of all the wannabe enlightened ones. There was also something new—but not really new: I was starting to feel my urge to make art again. I wanted to express myself and share the wisdom I had gathered on my spiritual path.

I hung out at the Santa Fe Public Library. I borrowed their video camera and began shooting. I edited all the stuff I transferred from reel to reel—stuff shot by Keith Haring and slides from my childhood. I booked the theatre at the Center For Contemporary Arts. I had a popular New Age recording artist James Oliver create a soundtrack. I called the performance "Drowning In The Light" to spoof Shirley MacLaine's book, *Dancing in the Light*.

It was around this time that I read a book by Jose Arguelles called *The Mayan Factor: Path Beyond Technology*. Arguelles proposed that August 17, 1987, was a significant date, which he identified as the Harmonic Convergence. The event signaled the final time period of the Old Age, according to the Mayan calendar, which was predicted to end on December 21, 2012. I was excited and inspired to attend a town hall meeting about the significance of the Harmonic Convergence. The auditorium was packed; people were enthusiastic about going to various sacred sites and meditating to usher in the New Age. I showed up alone, feeling skeptical about the significance of this date. I was weary of people showing up *en masse* to Chaco Canyon in northern New Mexico—Chaco Canyon is a very sensitive ecological area that supports ruins of the ancient Anasazi people.

As I sat and listened to a panel of psychics, astrologers, and New Age gurus, I became frustrated with all the projections and predictions. One of the psychics predicted there would be massive earth changes. All of a sudden, I could feel my metabolism speed up and everything began to appear in slow motion. Before I knew it, I was standing up shouting, "Is anyone going to Orion?" The entire auditorium went motionless. It was as if time and space were frozen. Time had stopped. And, yes, the way it appeared to me was as if I had hit the pause button. Not knowing what had moved me to do such a thing, I had a feeling that some force was working through me. With the panel frozen and the audience speechless, the moderator declared the event concluded.

What had happened? My blurting out a bizarre question should not have abruptly ended the panel discussion. I remember walking out of the auditorium. People seemed to be in a trance. A radio interviewer for the local public radio station stuck a microphone in my face and asked me if I believed anything was going to happen on this date. My response was, "We are waking up from a collective dream. This is simply an alarm clock."

Zero-Point Fusion

I was starting to believe, more and more, that the experiences I was having—which I identified as "being in the zero-point"—were precursors for a collective zero-point experience when the entire earth would experience a moment of non-time. It was as if we were heading toward that zero-point, and the Harmonic Convergence was an indicator of this universal shift.

My hand should have been badly burned in the wood stove. I should have been swept to my death forging the rushing river. My spontaneous outburst should not have stopped a conference. The universe was showing me how it seems to rearrange itself to reflect my thoughts and emotions, how my metabolism speeds up before I have a zero-point experience. Each time I accessed this zero-point gap of pure nothingness, I experienced an alteration of the outer material world's so-called physical laws. I needed answers. I needed quiet.

I found myself driving out to a small village called Galisteo, led there by spirit and the vague memory of hearing about some petroglyphs. I passed one of the few businesses—the Light Institute where Shirley MacLaine did her regression therapy. I saw a van parked on the side of the road, and watched as a young hippie-looking dude tucked under a barbwire fence. I pulled my car over and slipped under the fence to explore. On the top of a ridge, I discovered several petroglyphs, including one with what looked like a UFO with a strand of DNA descending. Was it possible that these native ancestors knew things we modern minds didn't even know about the origin of life on this planet? Perhaps they knew that our Sisters and Brothers from the Sky seeded our genetics here in the fertile earth?

This place became my power spot, as I would imagine flying across the basin by breathing in a circular breath. One day sitting on top of the ridge, looking down on the Galisteo Basin, I realized I had been there before in a dream. I recollected a dream that thousands of native people from many tribes descended from the hills and mountains to meet in a big open basin just like this one. I felt sad that this sacred land was privately owned and surrounded by barbwire. But glad it was mostly a secret.

As I sat on the highest boulder on the ridge I asked the Great Spirit for a vision. As I let go of my mind my breath naturally entered a figure-eight pattern that got smaller and smaller until it dissolved into a single point. And it was if my mind dissolved into infinity and eternity—that there was this point before time and space. Then I saw three stars in a triangle pointing down and knew this was an important symbol for me.

Living in Northern New Mexico was very grounding but I was getting restless. I felt I was hiding from a more conventional lifestyle as I had much disdain for modern civilization. I knew if I stayed in New Mexico I would lose my greater ambitions and fade into the earthen landscape, maybe even live in a tee pee and grow my own food and herbal medicine.

Somehow there was this gaping hole in my heart. I felt like my quest for solitude and spiritual awakening had bypassed the notion of settling down and living a normal life. Each time I asked myself, "What would that normal life even look like?" I would feel this tremendous energy surround me and show me there is a bigger role for me in the world. My message, as I meditated into the zero-point, was that it was time to reset my direction and unfold a new chapter in my life.

Then I had a vision that I was here to tell stores and that I should move to Los Angeles and make movies. I went to the library and discovered they had the Los Angeles phone book. It was so overwhelming I put it back on the shelf and opened up the San Diego phone book. Before I knew it I found myself a job as an art therapist in a medical center in San Diego and was heading west—again.

CHAPTER SIX: SUPERCONDUCTIVE

"For you
There might be another star
But through my eyes the light of you is all I see"
—Stevie Wonder

San Die Ego

San Diego was just what the doctor ordered. I found a converted garage to rent a few blocks from Swami's Beach in Cardiff-by-the-Sea and worked four days a week at the medical center running therapy groups on the children and adolescents acute psychiatric units. The hospital setting was unique for me as it was designed for short-term stays and meeting lots of interesting people—many with tragic stories and life-long psychiatric hospitalizations.

As I lead groups implementing such tools as art therapy, psychodrama and guided imagery—I discovered I had a special gift to help teens see their inner treasures.

Working the adolescent unit, I found many groups were focused on issues around suicide, as quite a few of the patients at anytime were in there for suicidal attempts or suicidal ideation. I also learned that I had to be smarter than the teenage existential mindset.

One of my favorite guided imagery exercises unfolded as a 14-year-old boy spent 10 minutes arguing why he has the right to end his emotional and psychological suffering by swallowing as many pills as he wished. And that he hated therapists, which he called "the rapists." After he decided to take a rest and the whole group fell into a moment of silence, I could feel there was much deeper contemplation going on in those adolescent minds.

That's when I told them all to close their eyes and imagine they were dead, floating down a tunnel of white light and being transported into this brilliant space. And then they enter this room filled with light and a man with flowing white hair, and they notice they are in a circle of young people. And then the man with the flowing beard says, "Are you ready to share your feelings around why you killed yourself? Oh no you can't escape your feelings. As we all find out in life that... the only way out is in!"

One time I was working on the acute psychiatric adult unit and a gentleman came to my group who spoke freely about his multidimensional problem. He said that he was living in-between dimensions and that I knew what he was talking about. Finally, I admitted that he was right except for the difference between he and I was that I was not telling anybody about it.

The Download Of Spiritual Voltage

Things were shifting with the people I was working with. I could feel an invisible force working through me. I knew I needed to go deeper into meditation. I began trading sessions with a woman who was one of the major Reiki healers in the area. She shared with me that the night before she was going to give me the attunements, a strong light shined down from the sky lighting up her entire bedroom. She then shared with me that she was guided to give me the highest level of Reiki attunements she was trained in.

As she was attuning me by projecting her hands toward my head, I had a flash of that same radiant symbol that fired into my mind atop the ridge in New Mexico. As this symbol, three points of light in a triangle facing downward appeared, I felt the moment of non-time and non-space as if all electromagnetism ceased. And I felt this symbol represented my breath fused into the state of wholeness and identified it as the "Fusion" symbol. The next day I wrote these words on a piece of paper: "Whole Light Fusion"—which is the state of perfect harmony and unity. The "Whole Light" is the still Light at the center of every particle of Creation. Whole Light Fusion is the awareness that Creator is inside all of Creation.

Fusion is the energy of the stars, as well as the force present during conception of life. At the center of every atom is a strong positive charge—the will to unite. This is the true "Yoga" (yoga means to unite with the source within). Union is the power of love, and love is the cohering agent within all form. When you breathe into your heart center and feel the unity of Creator and Creation, your Heart will enter a more coherent state. The heart as the master oscillator in the body produces the strongest electromagnetic signal, which permeates every cell in the body.

Within the year I had developed Whole Light Fusion into an entire system of personal transformation that worked to unify the fragmented aspects of self and dissolve the illusion of separation. It also was an energy work that was about catalyzing instead of healing that simply allows the Light to flow through you into others. It needed form and structure and I was to be the scribe. I needed to share this with others.

As I learned to breathe in a powerfully fluid way, information would come to me and then I would search the libraries to discover many times that the information I was receiving was beyond what I could have known without scientific training. I found myself on a deep research quest to verify the information I received. I became a monk reading up to 10 books at a time.

I discovered Eastern teachings informing me how advanced yogic breathing techniques can produce secretions in the brain that strengthen the human energy systems, resulting in the elimination of degeneration of the whole body. This secretion, called "amirdha," may be a substance that is the result of biological transmutation. Biological transmutation refers to the transmutation of the atomic or chemical elements, as they are commonly known in the periodic table. This is a sign that the human being is very much like the caterpillar in metamorphosis, and can consciously form his or her wings out of the molten substance of consciousness.

What is being suggested is that human beings are capable of experiencing the process of transfiguration, which was not exclusively available to Jesus. Transfiguration is a word mostly associated with Christ, yet other biblical figures such as Enoch experienced a transfiguration of the flesh. Perhaps this is what Christ meant when he spoke the words, "The flesh is weak, but the spirit is willing."

Superconductor Of Life Energy

I had wondered since I was a small child if there was electricity in my body like my friends inside the TV. What I had discovered was that we are actually conducting electricity into our cells through our breath. For some reason, every time I went into meditation I saw this flow of Light through my body and heard a voice in my head saying investigate superconductivity. So off I went to the UC Berkeley library and back home with every book about superconductivity. There was very little regarding Biological Superconductivity but I did discover a few things.

So what is superconductivity? Superconductivity is the conduction of energy without any resistance, therefore eliminating energy loss. In superconductivity, electrons pair up into couples without actually touching, and they adopt a common shared motion. This perfect cooperation results in a total elimination of the disorderly collisions that are the cause of resistance and energy loss.

Imagine the electricity flowing through the wires in your house. The electricity is composed of electrons that bounce around and collide with each other. In contrast, the electrons in a superconductor flow smoothly by cooperating with each other, therefore eliminating energy loss. I pondered these ideas and then I saw the equation at the heart of Whole Light Fusion:

Resistance = Stress = Breakdown

Imagine going through your day not resisting life and cooperating with everyone and moving in a smooth way? I had discovered a way to breathe that eliminates resistance. If you can feel the resistance and breathe through it into an ease of flow you will never get stressed. Stress will lead to breakdown whether you are talking about a gear or one's mental and emotional state. If anything, this sounded like a good metaphor for stress management.

But then I discovered more.

Herbert Frohlich (1968), one of the earlier researchers into biological superconductivity, theorized that the water in the cytoplasm of the cells is organized and is living water. In organized water, the water molecules become grouped into high-energy liquid crystalline structures. If organized water (commonly known as structured) is a liquid crystal, this suggests that the cytoplasmic water has the capacity to store information.

So I was right as a child—we were electric. If the cells are liquid crystal then we are like the very screen I am writing these words on. That the cells store information!

Now I wanted to know if cells could actually be superconducting. The late Freeman Cope, a scientist who worked at the Naval Research Lab, postulated that organic solids existing in the body might have superconductive properties. Cope believed that the constituents of nerve tissue (mostly cholesterol) may superconduct at physiological temperatures.

At the same time I began to discover correlating information in Eastern spiritual teachings. I learned the ancients knew about this biological superconductivity and referenced it in both the Rig Veda of Ancient India and the Taoist teachings from China.

I connected with a few leading edge scientists studying quantum biology and they confirmed that I was tapping into some pretty "out there" yet advanced knowledge.

At the moment a material becomes a superconductor, an energy field is generated that expels (forces out) all external magnetic influences including gravity. This would mean that the material would levitate, because levitation is the opposite of gravitation. This phenomenon is a result of something called the "Meisner Effect." When you read about "superconductors" in a science book, you will often see a picture of a levitating magnet illustrating the Meisner Effect.

If a human body can generate a Meisner field, then perhaps this may explain how select individuals throughout history exhibited supernormal powers like the ability to levitate and move objects with their mind. Maybe we lost these abilities as we allowed the density of the earth experience to grind us down. There is so little we really know of our hidden potential.

We take aging and death for granted as we allow life to grind us down. It always seems like things are falling apart. In time, rocks will disintegrate into sand, and in a shorter time, the treads on you car tires will wear down to nothing. The second law of thermodynamics (known as entropy) relates to the movement from order to disorder within systems over time. The higher the entropy in a system. the greater the disorder. Entropy is mirrored to us in our world through inanimate matter.

Although decay and death seems inevitable for the human body, it is interesting to know that biological systems are unique exceptions to the process of entropy—many aspects of biological functioning exhibit negative entropic properties. The highly entropic nature of the environment does take its toll on the biology. And in truth, we begin to age the moment we are born into this world.

Light Streams

I was beginning to see that I was tapping into the possible next stage of human evolution where we are able to superconduct life energy without resistance and focus on our bodies as Light. I had a vision that we will begin to experience ourselves become less dense and more luminous.

I read how opening to the Inner Light through meditative practices can actually amplify photons in your brain. The brain and nervous system can become sensitive to higher Light, because the cilia in the ventricles of the brain are constructed like the rods of the eye. These cilia are like fibers that attune to the Light.

So I imagined that without resistance, you awaken the potential of the brain to expand to new dimensions of the universal intelligence. It is common knowledge that we only use a small portion of our brainpower, yet we have the hardware (neural pathways) to accommodate a greater expansion of consciousness. So I figured that we would discover how to access these new pathways.

I discovered the work of Stuart Hameroff—who ended up 20 years later in the film *What The Bleep*. Harmeroff postulated that microtubules, the geometric lattices of proteins that compose the skeletons of the cells of the body, seem to fit the model of a vessel that transports the life energy in the form of coherent photons. I saw them as a physical constituent to the energy pathways that the Eastern sciences call *nadis*. The 72,000 nadis are the channels circulating *prana* (life energy) in your body. The microtubules are like a biological fiber optic system that delivers coded information.

Most neurobiologists focus on the synapses of the nervous system. But I perceived that each individual is a woven tapestry of light fibers with nodal points that absorb and radiate the Light of the higher realms. The nadis (as etheric energy pathways) interface with the meridian system described in ancient oriental medicine of which in which acupuncture is an aspect.

Both the meridians and nadis are circulatory systems interfacing with the grosser physical circulatory systems such as the microtubules and nervous system. Actually, all of these energetic pathways interpenetrate each other in the whole bio-energetic system commonly referred to as a human being. All of these essential life energy pathways flow out of the higher dimensional consciousness streams.

And then there was my experience as I began to teach Whole Light Fusion in small groups. I would visualize Light flowing through each person and as they breathed deeper in a more fluid way, I would feel as if they were becoming more radiant. I thought about the lighting fixture switches I used to turn up in the lighting store. As I turned the dial, the filament in the bulb became brighter and brighter. Then I started hearing people in the workshop share similar experiences about their cells glowing. I began to feel that Whole Light Fusion was a way of amplifying the flow of life energy in the cells. Turning up the dimmer switch and radiating the Light from within each cell!

And the thought I had that the human body is like a television set picking up the broadcast of our soul felt validated. It began to look as a possible scientific model presented by former Stanford University professor, Dr. William Tiller (1997) who 20 years later would also be a star in the film *What The Bleep*. Tiller presents a very comprehensive hypothesis in which he has used geometry to model grid structure that forms a matrix for the holographic projection of Divine mind. He calls this model the "simulator" and relates it to a huge ten-dimensional television set. His model fits very closely with my initial intuitive sensing that our Soul's are broadcast from a higher dimension into this dreamtime we call reality.

Tiller's model maps out a perfect crystalline lattice where the conversion of Divine mind (flowing as consciousness) is converted into the subtle energies that eventuate into material manifestation. As previously mentioned, this is because the conversion from consciousness to energy occurs at nodal points.

If an individual were to become more polarized to spirit than matter, perhaps they could absorb the universal Light substance directly. If one person has been documented to live off of universal Light, then all people could exist living off the Light. Remember, we eat the cow, which eats the grass, which eats the sun (photosynthesis). The sun is a step-down transformer for the Light descending from the galactic core. How can someone actually metabolize Light and nourish the body? I believe the study of biological superconductivity will give us greater understandings into this matter.

Many of us don't want to watch it in ourselves, but in time, as the aging process endures, cells move from the perfect order at birth to degeneration. For example, diseases such as cancer illustrate how chaos and destruction of the cells resulting later in many individual's lives. Our collective mind is imprinted with the common belief of aging and death, proven by the noticeable decay and inevitable death of those who age around us. These beliefs are centered on the experience of being separate from the Light of the Creator. This is evident in the belief of having to die to "go to God." By being cut off from the Eternal Light of Creation one literally experiences their self down here in this waiting room between heaven and hell.

CHAPTER SEVEN: DARK MIRROR

"Dark star crashes, pouring its light into ashes
Reason tatters, the forces tear lose from the axis"
—The Grateful Dead

Nomad

The early 1990s brought some serious winds of change. It started with uprooting my life in San Diego to be with a tall blonde chiropractor on the East Coast. She attended one of my Whole Light Fusion events and we *had instant false soulmate recognition.* We knew each other from another place—most likely called karma. We talked on the phone every night for hours and she visited me in California for a weekend of romance, confirming or rather colluding our soulmate myth. By the time I drove back across the country to be with her, her story was changing.

Within two weeks of landing on her doorstop—she determined she "was not ready." I remember walking out the door with such rage and pain in my heart. I had no keys or wallet and no shoes. I walked at least one mile down the dirt road in the middle of nowhere and stopped in my tracks and began to laugh. I felt this peace rush over me with a feeling that I could be walking barefoot forever in a state of pure ecstasy and need nothing anymore. I needed no one. And I ended up with nothing.

I found myself stuck without any money and nowhere to live. For some time I lived in the "healing room" at the back of a metaphysical bookstore. Once I was able to get my life on track, I was able to set up several Whole Light Fusion workshops across the country. I found myself living out of my Honda Civic, and on the adventure of a lifetime—it's called the unknown. I truly had no home-base. I had one key on my key ring. If someone asked me where I lived—in a semi-joking manner—I replied, "My drivers license says California. But honestly not sure where I will eventually wind up."

My adventures began with a Whole Light Fusion workshop I did at a Christian retreat in Florida. I had met an artist/singer young woman who caravanned with me. She and I drove along side and even camped out together pitching our tents next to each other. She headed over toward Tennessee to hopefully sing in a club in Nashville and serendipity delivered me to places literally beyond my wildest dreams.

The Ghost Of Walter Russell

While traveling through Virginia I discovered that I was not far from Swannanoa Villa built in 1912 fashioned after Italian Renaissance architecture—it was leased to Walter Russell and his wife Lao from 1949 until their deaths. Walter Russell was perhaps one of the greatest minds of his times. His book *The Secret Of Light* slipped into my hands in 1980 and remains to this day one of my most treasured books.

I thought there was a museum there so I looked up the directions and headed to the estate. I was welcomed at the door by the caretaker who lived there with his wife. He informed me there was no longer a museum.

Saddened that I made it all the way there and could not go inside, I expressed my disappointment. After letting the caretaker know I had read all of Walter Russell's books many times and that I felt *The Secret Of Light* as the most important book I had ever read, suddenly the caretaker took a moment to think and then said, "Come on in and we will give you the tour."

The second story to the villa was closed off to the public, but the ground floor had many of Russell's paintings and diagrams of the structure of physical reality including what some could describe as his own periodic elements chart. Walter Russell had many relationships with many of the most important figures of modern history including Edison, Tesla and Teddy Roosevelt.

I felt compelled to tell the caretaker the experience I had when I was in my mid-twenties. I shared with him and his wife how I was sick with a high fever and fell asleep with *The Secret of Light* on my lap and then suddenly I felt I was awake and Walter Russell was in the room in his Light body. I said the next thing I knew I was touching the ceiling as if I had levitated. Then suddenly it felt as if I was dropped from the ceiling to the bed—yet I was there all along as well.

They were in awe of my deep connection with the spirit of Walter Russell. And the caretaker said, "We have something we rarely share with anyone." He walked up the staircase to a landing with a pipe organ. He said Walter Russell wrote this music correlating music harmonics with DNA sequencing. The caretaker played the sheet music and I stood below the staircase with a frame drum I brought out from my hatchback—playing a single heartbeat that resonated throughout the massive entryway of the villa. I was in a dream world and that night they invited me to spend the night on the second floor in the guest bedroom. They had never invited anybody to sleep in this room. I slept in the same bed Tesla slept in when he visited.

When you are a nomad living in the moment, new experiences show up that are truly beyond one's wildest dreams. The next morning I said my goodbyes to the caretaker and his wife. It was time for me to head toward Ohio for a weekend Whole Light Fusion workshop.

Sweating With The Sun Dancers

I rarely pick up hitchhikers in this day and age—who would be insane enough to pick up a hitchhiker? The last time I picked up a hitchhiker was in the Everglades. He had long hair and a beard and was wearing a big quartz crystal around his neck. He did not attack me, rape me or rob me, but rather inspired me in a very aggressive way to hike with him. We found a path and I followed him into the dense sticky air and through the swampy forest. Ten minutes into the forest we had stumbled into swarms of mosquitoes and the crystal dude ran ahead at least 100 feet, when I saw him sinking. It was unlike the movies when people sink in quicksand, but he was sinking in what appeared to be quicksand. He got out and we turned back only to encounter a family of alligators.

So here I was energized by my experience at Walter Russell's estate, and driving alone on the back roads and I see a hitchhiker. This one seemed to have a necklace of long feathers and I found myself pulling over to pick him up.

What was I doing? I was making room in an already full car for the hitchhiker and his backpack. And the feathers he wore were from road kill. He turned out to be on his way to a Native American Sun Dance—the kind where the dancers pierced themselves. Yet he was not Native American—he was very white. He convinced me to take him to the Sun Dance as it was in Ohio and on the way to where my workshop was being held. It was getting late and it seemed like this place was truly in the middle of nowhere. Which is exactly where it was.

By the time we finally got to the site it was dusk. As I was about to pull out of the dirt parking lot, I noticed someone I had known in New Mexico. I got out of the car and hugged his sweaty body and the next thing he was inviting me to spend the night. If you were not there to Sun Dance—you were there to support it. Much work was needed. What was I getting myself into? I was ready to say thank you and keep moving when I somehow was also invited to sit in the sweat lodge with the Sun Dancers.

I had been to at least a dozen sweat lodges over the years. Each time they do a round for each direction and open the flap and air out the lodge before bringing more hot rocks off the fire and into the center of the lodge. In this lodge there was only one round with rocks coming in and the flap staying closed. For the Sun Dancers that have been fasting and training themselves to overcome the hardship through transcendence, this was a warm-up exercise (literally). For me, I had a vision of Grandma's chicken soup where the chicken skin slides off the chicken in the boiling pot of soup. I felt my skin would slide off the bone. After the lodge we were all hosed down with cold water as it started to rain.

I could not put up my tent in the dark rainy night so I accepted the invitation to share a tent with my friend from New Mexico. After 30 minutes of smelling his dirty body, feeling the rain leak in on my side creating a puddle, and listening to him snore—I bailed into the dark rainy night to find my car and make a getaway.

After several months of teaching workshops crisscrossing the USA, I began to feel this emptiness. I was in my thirties and alone—without a home. I began to feel tired of being someone's guest. I was not sure where my next home would be. I wondered what my life would have been like if I did not have this desperate search for higher meaning gnawing at me. If I had taken over my father's business selling lightning fixtures instead of driving around the country selling the "Experience of Light."

Finding My Split-Level Paradise

Everything we focus on we manifest in some form. After four months on the road living out of my Honda Civic hatchback, I settled in for a month at a student's ranch in Arizona. It was during this time that I had connected with a woman I had a crush on when I met her ten years earlier in Marin. Before I knew it, I was driving back to California. We hung out for a few weeks and realized we were not the best match. She was older than I, and with grown kids. I was beginning to feel that having a child was something I wanted to experience.

The universe does listen to your deep desires, even when you least expect them. As I was now back to my nomadic search for my next step in life, I decided to go to one of my favorite hiking trails in Marin leading out to the coast. As I sat in my car contemplating my aimless search for meaning in my life, I noticed a woman sitting in her car apparently meditating. On her dashboard was a hawk feather. I was now intrigued and found myself watching her meditate.

Suddenly, it was if she could physically feel me and turned her head to make eye contact with me. As we both got out of our cars at the same time to gather ourselves for the hike, I noticed that I recognized her. Katrina and I had met six years earlier when I came to meet her with her now ex-husband about the work they were doing using healing technology and crystals. Since her divorce Katrina was writing about *"getting in touch with the soul of the unborn child."* I was intrigued.

As we began to walk and talk I realized Katrina's most important focus in life was having a child. By the end of the hike she clearly stated, "I don't even want to start a relationship with anyone that is not ready to have a child." We dated and it was not long before I found myself throwing away my briefs and buying boxers to optimize my sperm. I was now only six months down the road from the meeting at the hiking trail, and had been chosen to father a child for a woman writing about "conscious conception." She was very psychic and had tuned into the name of this child already—knowing it was a girl—and it was!

We agreed to marry and gave birth to a beautiful baby girl. We bought a split-level house in a development reminding me of the split-level house I grew up in. I had finally achieved the dream my parents had for me. I was blessed to have a life where I was able to spend time with my daughter during her entire childhood. Cooking dinners, creating bizarre puppet shows to entertain my daughter and myself and even going to school meetings. Eventually I got a job working with a visionary businessman and co-authored books and traveled doing conferences. We created a start-up and I was the head of publishing.

Katrina and I began to drift apart. The tension around finances and our differences of opinions on so many matters stirred us up as both of us were projecting our experiences on each other in the dark mirror. At times I would see her face change and could feel a sense of ancient karma, as if we had been at war with each other in a past life and in this life we both had the ability to drive each other insane.

With all this tension in my marriage and the company I was working for running out of gas—at the same time flying to the East Coast to assist with my mom's health as it seemed that she was in the early stages of Alzheimer's. My dad could not see that she needed to be treated by a neurologist and that if she confused a coffee cup with a soup bowl she could confuse a red light from a green light and needed to stop driving.

I starting to feel abandoned by the women in my life. I needed to feel my own feminine side—my "inner mother." One Sunday I went to go see a spiritual teacher that was described as a "Holy Mother" from India. We sat in mediation and tears streamed down my face. I went to receive a message from her. I felt a love I was craving and she blessed me to heal my karma. On my way home I got a shocking call from my sister who informed me that my mother had a stroke and could be dead in a short time.

That night I hopped on a red-eye. All night I was praying for her soul and praying that she would still be alive. I was listening to the Divine Mother on my iPod singing the Gayatri Mantra. I had a vision of two birds crossing each other in the sky. When I got to the Charlotte airport I had a lay-over and was about to board the plane to Tampa when my sister called—they did not know how much longer they could keep her alive.

On my flight from Charlotte to Tampa I prayed deeply that I could see her before she left this physical world and somewhere mid-flight as I was dozing off, I had a feeling that raised the hair on my arms. I could feel my mother left and was passing me like we were the two birds in the vision. When my plane landed my cell phone rang I had missed her by 15 minutes. But I knew her spirit was soaring.

After my mother's death and the fall of the Twin Towers months after her death, I discovered my job as a publisher had turned to dust as expected. Finances got tight and fighting in my marriage got worse and worse. A rage that had been burning inside of me like a fire never really went out—it just needed oxygen. Little comments were reminding me of the nagging side of mother and I was suffocating. I was trying to grieve with the pressure of making money. I began to market myself as a consultant and started working with interesting new clients such as an ex-hedge fund manager wanting to write a book about the myth of money and security.

Splitting

The post 911 climate was a tough time for a leading-edge consultant. Eventually, I began to get more work consulting and traveling. In the first decade of the new millennium, I had two books published and spoke at conferences promoting the books. I was invited to speak to business consultants in Sydney and was thrilled as I always had a dream of going to Australia. I took a special excursion to Uluru, the Aboriginal name for Ayers Rock—the 600-million-year-old monolithic rock in the center of Australia.

It was on that trip that I had a profound dream. The dream was showing me that my marriage was becoming a dark mirror where I could not see my reflection any more because I had merged with her into this place of fear and blame. Every time we argued I saw myself in her. I saw the split in me. I saw the split in her. I felt that she was dreaming me and her version of me was not who I was. This dream showed me that I would be in danger if I stayed in the marriage.

Hoping a vacation could ease the tension, on one of my business trips to Sydney, I booked a flight with a layover in Fiji and booked my family a vacation as I would go on to Sydney and they would return home. On the second to last day in Fiji while playing tennis with my daughter, I injured my calf muscle. As I parted ways traveling on solo to Sydney, I was scared. I remembered a dream I had many years earlier that I went to the Outback and had no shoes and my feet were raw and bruised—I was aimlessly lost, internally and externally. And here I was traveling on to Australia on business and I could barely put any pressure on my leg.

Before my work in Sydney I was staying at a home on the bluffs overlooking the coastline of Byron Bay, and I was hobbling. My host was a woman who had built this dream house with her husband. He had gotten sick and passed away soon after the house was built. Doris was like an angel to me. She had a wonderful glass guesthouse in which many visiting authors and teachers stayed. She saw me hobbling and I proceeded to tell her how I hurt my leg. She called over a friend that was a retired osteopath.

The doctor was living on the property doing garden work and came over immediately with his tool belt on. He told me to take my pants off and I heard him gulp as I looked down and was shocked to see my leg purple from knee to toes. He was concerned I had thrombosis. I was due to fly back in four days. A 14-hour flight with thrombosis was not a good idea. I had not seen the color of my leg because I did not want to look. I could not handle that the entire lower leg was purple. I had this flash that I was going to die. I called my wife to share my feelings and get sympathy and she began to rip into me about money. I felt the end was near.

Doris came over to see if I needed anything. She asked if she could do some healing work on my leg. I was very open. Suddenly I thought that I was going to die. She told me to allow myself to feel this feeling. I had had it several times before. That if I died, that would be okay. That I would still exist!

It turned out that I had torn a muscle and finally gave my speech on my bum leg, taught a workshop and returned home. Things were so bad now in my marriage, that when I arrived home we were truly disconnected. And then we took a drive out to the seashore on Father's Day and we nearly died in a car accident. We were having a stupid argument about meaningless things, and I decided to turn the car around coming a hair's breadth from a head-on that would have killed us all. How many more warning signs did I need?

And then some wealthy friends of Katrina paid for us both to attend a human potential therapy called "The Program"– a 10-day wilderness retreat. No cell phone, no history. Just working out your stuff. The hope was that it would save our marriage. We had 12-hour days of intense psychological processing and I was starting to lose it. I could start to see how damaged I was from all of the processing—from all of the psychological and emotional emphasis that I had been immersed in. I was starting to hate all of it—sharing circles, hugs and endlessly crying by grown adults fixated on their pain from the past.

Then we were surprised one morning when we were told we would not be in the big hall processing, but instead going on a small excursion. We were driven in the van to a cemetery. It was an old cemetery and it was creepy. We were told to meditate on our mortality. I closed my eyes and had a vision that I had driven my car off a cliff and my daughter, who was 12 at the time, was so angry that I had killed myself that she smashed her prize possessions—ceramic flower fairies. I began to cry and feel that I had wasted my life always looking for the answer—and the program was only showing me the deeper pain I was feeling. I was trying to be accepted for who I was in life, not what someone wanted me to be. After Katrina and I did the retreat we both were clear our marriage was running out the meter.

Be careful what you meditate on especially when you are meditating on a cemetery, as several months after I did the program I was driving on a mountain road talking on the cell phone to Katrina and she was going on about money and I felt like a trapped animal and began screaming "What do you want my blood?" I was so enraged and out of my body with one hand on the wheel heading into a hairpin turn—and then I was in the zero-point. Time stood still and I had a flash of me meditating in the cemetery. This was a point where I could have gone off the road and off the cliff. But I put the phone down and put two hands on the wheel and drove home knowing this was the end!

I began to sleep downstairs and woke up with strange bruises on my body. I was worried that Katrina sleep-walked in the middle of the night and beat me; after all, she was now taking Ambien to sleep. I was ready to finally move out and began the oh-so painful process of splitting up the stuff with her. I began to fill boxes one morning and discovered blood on the box. I then discovered that blood was dripping from my nose. My nose bled for at least 20 minutes. Something was getting weird. Yet, I ignored it—"must just be stress" I said.

Within the week I started bringing boxes over to my new home—I took almost nothing from the 12-year marriage. Not a stitch of furniture, dishes, household goods, not even my tools. But, I was free—and I was exhausted from the move, schlepping boxes up three flights to my apartment. I went to take a shower and stripped off my clothes only to see a dark image in the mirror. At least 60% of the front of my body was mostly bruised.

CHAPTER EIGHT: 2012—END OF THE NEW AGE

"And in the end
The love you take
Is equal to the love you make."

The Beatles—The End

Bruised

In 2008 my full apocalypse happened in 3D–disease, divorce and debt. As I watched the Wall Street criminals proving the old adage that "the best way to rob a bank is to own it," and watched my soon to be ex-wife push harder in the divorce, I also discovered new bruises showing up on my body out of nowhere—many the size of pancakes. I became obsessed with bleeding to death too. Sometimes after flossing my teeth, my gums would just start bleeding and it would take half a pack of tissue before the bleeding would stop.

Then I learned how to control the bleeding by breathing into the area of the gum affected and turn it off. What I had learned by teaching Whole Light Fusion was if you breathe following a figure-eight pattern where there is no pause between the inhale and exhale, you can get into this fluid state of being. If you follow the figure-eight until it disappears into the center, then you can enter a state where it feels like you are not breathing at all, as if you are no longer in the duality of inhale and exhale. That is the state in which I stopped the bleeding. It was that zero-point where I disappeared into the arms of Creation and into the heart of ever particle.

And at the same time I would beat myself up for "creating this." This is one of the pitfalls of putting too much belief in the New Age concept that we "create our reality." Reality is happening in many dimensions of being. After all, life is a mystery partly because our brain cannot handle trying to understand the multiple dimensions of consciousness that we are working through in this one moment. That is why we need to understand that at the energy level of reality, things are malleable. But once they have manifested in physical reality, they are more challenging to shift.

But, back now to my health issues. I realized I finally needed to face Western medicine. My acupuncturist told me I had better get my blood drawn and have it sent to the lab. I was confused about what was going on in my body and scared to death of the idea of a bone marrow biopsy. Trying to get some sleep was a nightmare. My t-shirt would be soaked with perspiration and when I did wake up, I'd be ruminating on death. I still was not certain what was wrong with me. They could not rule out leukemia until I ended up getting the bone marrow biopsy.

As it turned out, I was diagnosed with an autoimmune blood condition called ITP where my antibodies are marking and destroying my platelets. Platelets are the clotting factor in blood. In a normal micro-litter of blood there should be between 140,000 to 400,00 platelets. My platelets were starting to fall below 20,000. When I was under 10,000 the doctors and I were seriously concerned. What's remarkable though is that with 90 percent of my platelets being destroyed at any given time, those surviving were becoming super platelets. Under the microscope they were large. It was like all I had left on my defensive line were a couple of very big tough guys protecting me from turning into a puddle of blood.

By having to receive platelet transfusions, my lifelong fear of IVs and receiving someone else's blood cells transformed into gratitude to the generous donors who were keeping me alive. I had so many IVs in my arms that the first hospitalization left me with several bruises that looked like tattoos. An especially chilling one left three dots in the shape of a triangle—the fusion symbol.

I knew that controlling my bleeding was not a life-long solution as I was concerned I could have an injury more severe than a bleeding gum. Yet I continued to live my life knowing that at any point I could have killed myself riding horses in Mexico, shooting over waves in a Zodiac boat, or just having my airbag accidentally go off in a parking lot fender bender.

As I reached out to many of my old friends, I felt like I was trying to hold on to some facsimile of my former life. It truly was a time for letting go, but my life seemed so incomplete. There was so much I had on my plate still, but hanging over my head now were worries about platelets dissolving into the void. And the death of who I believed I was—a healthy, holistic, awakened Light worker.

The divorce was brutal, according to my lawyer "unusually so." My business went bust and the bank froze my business line of credit. In 2008, the year that many homeowners foreclosed on their homes also brought bank bailouts and urban tent camps! I figured the follow up to the my last book, *The Flip* would be one called *Flip Out* as I expected the financial securities meltdown to leave people with little to feel secure about.

My daughter was 14 then and she was my greatest joy. But I worried she would be traumatized by the divorce, And even though she seemed so mature and understanding, I also could not let myself become a sick person. I knew I must stay well to watch her become a woman, as well as to fulfill my missions in life.

I began meditating and reprogramming my mental state, visualizing my platelets flourishing. Visualizing my antibodies laying down their arms. Visualizing my body stopping attacking itself. I would often lay awake, many a night breathing into the nothingness, asking the angels for grace and strength. I imagined I was accessing the zero-point and activating my DNA. I reasoned too that if I could heal myself, I could tell my story to the world. I figured maybe that was why I got this dreadful condition. Then I realized everything that we get in life must be part of the curriculum. As if we have general aspects of our soul that we need to develop and the details are just filled in by life.

Since I felt I had been given this esoteric information, my job was to create a context for the healing work I saw taking place with Whole Light Fusion. After all, I had heard from countless people who had amazing healing experiences with Whole Light Fusion. I never asked for testimonials, they just came unsolicited and were described by people who had no scientific context for the physiological shifts they experienced.

I felt as though I was being tested by the angels of healing to see how I could heal and transform my own complex medical challenge. To see if I could awaken from the overwhelming emotional hijacking from within that whispered the dreadful thought that it was all a delusion and I would die as a dreamer without any tangible contribution to the world with the exception of my awesome daughter.

I felt like I was an imposter thinking I could shift my physiological state just by breathing and visualizing. But, I also knew deep inside my being that one day I would pop out of this disturbance in my energy field. I could see it when I closed my eyes.

I could see its imprint at the subatomic level where there is only energy and information and no matter.

When I was developing Whole Light Fusion, I started to feel that all disease was like static on a radio or like a maladjustment of one's antenna to their Higher Self—a glitch in their TV signal. That genetic predisposition to a disease was nothing but some bad code that traveled up the gene pool. That genetic material was the physical component to its energetic counterpart—the software to the genetic hardware.

I thought about employing homeopathy, radionics, acupuncture and all of the systems to tune one's energy frequency, but my condition was deeper than my energy body. None of those systems worked. My autoimmune condition is at a deeper cellular level. I needed to work with herbs I decided. Powerful herbs! So I began to research on the internet, wanting to trust that there was a natural regime that would clear this glitch from my DNA.

But the endless stream of money spent on herbal supplements, tinctures, and teas never moved the needle on my condition. I kept getting referrals to the "real deal" regarding healers. One healer told me that my blood was going through a mutation. That she knew other "Light workers" who were experiencing low platelets too. Another told me that extraterrestrials were "working on me."

As I became more and more turned off to free advise, I still figured I would find a natural cure. I sought out more naturopaths and acupuncturists. They helped me in many ways, but usually it was always more and more herbs and supplements. Chinese herbs you crush and drank in tea reminded me of the concoctions I imbibed with Don Eduardo in Peru. Then there was papaya leaf extract—it was known to raise the platelet levels—that I made triple strength; it was so bitter I put several spoonfuls of honey in just to drink it down.

Everyone I met had a solution they swore by. I was given a mat that generated an electromagnetic field and it was supposed to transform my blood. I was given special essential oils that when rubbed on my chakras cleared the negative energy. Eventually though I did not want to hear any more unsolicited advice from Light workers, healers or intuitive consultants, and I did not want any information about the next new miracle product that required membership and business building kits.

One thing surprising to me was when I had a sudden craving for red meat. I had not eaten red meat for close to 20 years but I thought I had better listen to my body. So I found myself in my new rental condo, settled into my IKEA décor, looking out at the small balcony where I had my little gas grill smoking out the entire east end of the complex. My balcony faced an open field at the other end. Just beyond that field was an organic chicken processing plant. What I did not know when I moved in was that the chicken delivery was in the wee hours of the morning so those idling trucks ready to deliver totally hip organic chickens to their truly organic slaughter kept me up every night.

My father was now 90 years old and exhibiting the early signs of ALS. His pain that his son had a blood disorder concerned him more than his decreased ability to achieve any fine motor skills. My sister and I spoke every day about either, or more often both, my dad's ALS and my platelets. I was like "Mr. Glass." I was fragile, but my dad, he was a fall waiting to happen. We got him 24-hour care so he could stay in his home. It was a time of deep sadness and fear. As for me, any little bump of an elbow could create a bruise the size of a large pancake. I felt that I had a curse.

Woman Of My Dreams

Back in the early nineties, soon after I followed the tall blonde chiropractor to the East Coast and was marooned–I met a woman who was a healer. She primarily used hypnosis. In one of my sessions I had a vision of a younger woman with long brown hair and slender legs wearing a white skirt and cowboy boots. She was standing on a hillside. This vision stayed with me as I traversed the country a couple of years later in my little Honda Civic and my one key looking for my next home.

By 1993, I finally made it back west. The first place I checked out as a possible home base was Boulder, Colorado. Boulder is a New Age Mecca with lots of organic food, healing schools, and massage therapists. After a short time I continued down to Santa Fe only to discover it was not greeting me with open arms this time around. Then by late August I found myself at a horse ranch in Arizona teaching workshops and watering down the horses. Serendipity arrived with a visit from the rancher's friend who shockingly happened to be a woman I had met in Marin and was attracted to 10 years earlier. How was this possible?

She was driving back to Northern California and I went along for the ride. And before I knew it, I was back in Marin with my car seeing if the two of us had something worth pursuing. And when I realized it was not the right relationship, I was ready to leave. As a matter of fact, I was preparing to leave California when I went on that auspicious hike and met my ex-wife Katrina, the woman I would father my daughter with.

The universe is always Divine perfection, and clearly having this child in my life has made me a better person. But, here I was 13 years later, divorced and feeling rather hopeless in life. I had long forgotten about the vision of the young woman on the hillside with the long flowing hair, white skirt, slender legs and cowboy boots. Now I was just looking for a companion. Someone I could relate to and just have fun with.

How would I meet her? Would I need to join a group? That was something I did not really enjoy—I can't stand name tags and sharing circles. I was ready to break out from the usual. I thought I would be happy if there was just someone I could date.

So, I was convinced by my daughter to join an online dating site. After several unsuccessful dates and feeling truly discouraged and wondering if it's best to be alone... I met her. Her name was Diana.

Only online could a Jewish liberal artist type from New York make the perfect match with a country music loving woman with Native American roots. She was 10 years younger than me and had been meditating since she was 12 years old. Diana was unlike anyone I had ever known, particularly in the sense that she was more truly authentic because she seemed like such a pure soul. She never experimented with drugs either, whereas I had been a Timothy Leary protégé inner space explorer.

Yet, she did not judge me and was open to learning from me. And I was open to learning from her too, though after much resistance. It is hard to cleanse oneself of past relationships especially when you are going though a divorce. But, she had been through one and helped me see it all from a higher perspective. As I was looking at the trees, she was there looking at the forest and reminding me that "these are all just moments that will pass and you will be at a different place." I saw how she constructed reality from a different vantage point, and by that time, rather than resist, I allowed myself to see from her perspective and to actually feel from her perspective. This was true empathy, true devotion. This was new for me.

I began reading to Diana from my esoteric books before going to sleep each night with her. She just listened, lying in my arms. I took her to spiritual gatherings and other New Age scenes. One night she came with me to a party and said, "I must be honest with you. I can't stand all these circles where people share and weep and hug–it's kind of weird to me." Still, she was good about it and we walked into the party. There was great music and we were eating the raw food snacks having a nice chat with a friend when a Tibetan bowl rang and a circle was called. An hour later though after sitting in a half lotus with my leg cramping, we had witnessed enough sharing and supporting, we realized we had it with it all.

We both starting feeling like there was nothing we needed to do to experience our spirituality, or to have to share everything with everyone, when we wanted to just have fun. Our everyday Being was filled with ecstasy and I began to fall deeper in love with this woman. I felt so loved and cared for. Somebody accepting me as I was—low platelets and all.

She and I both shared a vision that we had known each other for countless lives. We both had a vision that in another life we would meet each other on a hillside and would lay together on a blanket holding each other and feeling our two bodies as one. Was it a past life? Or, do we both share a reality in a parallel dimension that exists right here and now?

Time is an illusion of the mind. When you truly meet your soul mate you know you will never leave them because you never left them. It is like the blending of two colors. They create a third color that is an awesome merging of each others essence—like a chemist making perfume from two distinct flowers.

Months passed and we began to feel like hermits. About then, I felt obliged to go to a friend's birthday party. It turned out to get to the party we needed to hike out to a hillside for some kind of New Age gathering. As people formed a circle and I could see my sweetheart giving me the eye–I stopped and took notice of how beautiful she was inside and outside, noticing her hair glistening in the sun and her white skirt and cowboy boots. And there she was standing on a hillside in Northern California, with long brown hair blowing in the wind. Suddenly I knew she was the woman from my hypnosis experience—the woman of my dreams.

I knew she was the woman I wanted to spend my life with. We got married and went on a cruise to the Bahamas. I also introduced her to my then 92-year-old dad in Florida. He fell in love with my new wife and I was feeling blessed that he had the chance to get to know her. She got to experience his pure heart and we were blessed as a couple. I knew in my heart we would be together forever. This was a great healing experience from which he could leave this world knowing his son had found the woman of his dreams and would not be alone in life with a blood disease.

The other good news was my platelet count had began to rise out of extreme danger, so my dad could leave this world with some hope that I could live a healthy life. With his own health however, his ALS was progressing and he became less able to walk and function. Even though he had 24-hour care, there was a concern he would not be able to live in his home. My dad's greatest wish was not to have to go to assisted living and instead to live out the rest of his life in the home he shared with his wife for so many years.

Fly Me To The Moon

2011 was quite a year. My dad was losing the ability to speak and I was unsure if I would ever see him again as my daughter and I flew out to see him. When we arrived back home, I noticed I was bruised all over my body. I wondered if this deep sadness was having an effect on my platelets? Within a week I was in the hospital as my numbers were in the single digits. The doctors were worried I could internally bleed. Things got pretty bad and I was in and out of the hospital for a couple of weeks. They had me on such high doses of steroids—a treatment used for ITP—that I needed medicinal cannabis to sleep at night. But when the steroids were at the highest level and I was still bleeding I would be admitted again. It was a back and forth that became routine.

One time when I went back in I brought a jar of organic almond butter infused with cannabis oil. I made sandwiches that I ate with IVs in both arms. Then one night I woke up and saw my mother sitting in a chair in the room. She was coming for my father but wanted to let me know it was not my time. She was in the chair and then she disappeared.

For a moment, I felt the familiar comfort that my mother would always be there—because I came from her into this world, we would have a bond beyond death. For a moment, I forgot that she had been dead for 10 years, wondering how she got into the hospital room. Then I realized she may have been a dream, yet I was left with a feeling of comfort that went beyond that from the nurses, doctors and other caregivers—my mother was sending healing from Heaven.

With 1,200 ml. of liquid prednisone on one arm and a bag of platelets pumping in to my other arm, I thought of all the thousands of cells it took to make that bag of platelets. And I thought that I was truly connected to the world through my blood. And who were these people that donated blood enabling me to survive? And if I am connected to them I wanted to send love out through the quantum field to them alive or dead.

By Thanksgiving my numbers rose to a safe enough level and I was thrilled to share the news with my dad. He felt peaceful to know this. Then, within a week he fell and was in the hospital. I knew this was the end and I quickly flew to Florida. When I arrived he was in his hospital bed feeble and delirious. He was unable to swallow, therefore needed a feeding tube. At age 93 with progressed ALS, it was time for my dad to go home to his beloved wife.

My sister and her daughter flew down and I arranged to have hospice come to his home and transport him to his own space to pass from this world. The hospice nurses were like angels. They even had an aromatherapy diffuser, and a music therapist came with her guitar. With my hand on my father's heart and the music therapist playing his favorite song on acoustic guitar, *Fly Me To The Moon*, my dad took has last breath There I was by his side bringing one of his greatest desires to him—to die in his home with family.

After my father's death, I began to examine even more closely my life and my beliefs. I realized how I had rejected my father's materialistic view of reality and sought spiritual experiences as a way of affirming my Divine nature. I was in denial of my physical existence though, convinced life was a holographic projection and I was made of Light. I even produced a bumper sticker in the early nineties that said YOU ARE LIGHT! DRESSED UP IN MATTER. Yet here I was as human as I could be, more aware of the gift of the temporal life in a human body.

As the song goes, "Fly me to the moon...let me play amongst the stars." I had spent a couple of decades on this wild ride through the stars. Drumming under the New Mexican sky, standing in the flames in the land of the Incas, hungry for the Dreamtime, the return of the space brothers, 2012, the New Earth. My quest had lost its sheen. And I was starting to value the mundane and simple joys of material life. I began to see how I was programmed to believe that New Age people were evolutionary agents who were more spiritually advanced—that we were the 144,000 masters that would anchor the Light and usher the new dawn.

I began to see how I programmed myself to believe that modern Western medicine was evil and all they knew were drugs and surgery, and that the health insurance industry was a scam. For the two decades I spent exploring the spiritual dimensions prior to my first marriage, I had no health insurance. This disturbed my dad and when he questioned me my retort would be something like, "Buying health insurance is buying into disease." I felt that I had the natural ability to heal and basically was terrified by doctors and hospitals because I feared they were not to be trusted. I feared that the drug companies were trying to get everyone addicted to their pills so they could make billions.

Although some of this could be considered true, I was completely deluded by my fear of the medical establishment. I started to see how right my dad was about having medical insurance and how human I really was, even though I understood that I was made of vibration—that I was made of energy fields that were beneath the surface of physical form, even though on that surface I was bruised and vulnerable.

Yet, here I was approaching the end of the Mayan calendar, my parents both gone from the earth and facing uncertainty regarding my health. My mind would wander between visions of waking up one morning disease free and on the other end, suddenly internally bleeding to death. So, what is death anyway and how could I just live for the now? I was starting to feel disconnected to self-inquiry, to needing to do anything anymore. I learned to live with low platelets and to be thankful every day that I was alive and well.

The Day The New Age Ended

Because I have been in the publishing industry, I had been involved with consulting on several books about the mystical significance of 12-21-2012. One project I helped get published was written by Stephanie South about her partner Jose Arguelles and his prophetic journey with the forthcoming global transformation. Jose had been the person who came to Santa Fe and proclaimed the Harmonic Convergence of August of 1987 as a significant date based on his studies of the Mayan calendar. He was the person the media focused on as the guru behind the Convergence.

Now here it was over two decades later and just a couple of years from the "end of the Mayan calendar," and I was invited to dinner with Stephanie and Jose. Our conversation was exciting as they communicated how leaders from indigenous cultures were confirming we were entering a planetary shift of epic proportions. He reminded me of the passion I had about ushering in a cycle of human evolution. I had truly believed that the world we knew would collapse and new holistic systems and structures would rise up in place, yet here we were close to 2012 and it seemed like business as usual.

And then I met Steve Copeland, the filmmaker behind *Shift Of The Ages*—the story about Guatemalan Mayan spiritual leader Don Alejandro, or as most know him *'Tata.'* The message of the film was one of hope but also one of warning. I felt it was such an important film and did some consulting for Steve with the hope it would both be ready for Sundance 2012 and also become a must-see film for all those ready to hear the message. I felt that so many people were deluded about the Mayan calendar and Don Alejandro's message was so timely.

As a publisher of digital media e-books, I was hired to create a media e-book for my literary agent and friend William Gladstone. Bill had written a novel about 2012 called *The Twelve*, but had additionally authored a book with "Chicken Soup For The Soul" co-author Jack Canfield. That book, *The Golden Motorcycle Gang*, shared the visions of Canfield, Gladstone and Barbara Marx Hubbard as they related to the planetary birth that was to take place on this 2012 date. To me, 2012 was like the number set on the collective consciousness alarm clock, yet I knew most people would choose to hit the snooze button anyway.

What I knew inside was that the real pole shift was an internal movement from seeing the world through the lens of separation to seeing the world through a state of unified awareness. Yet, even though I sensed "nothing was going to happen" on December 21, 2012, I still felt compelled to be with others in a ritual of some sort on that day. The day was filled with activities ushering in this age of enlightenment. There were live streams of global events including one in LA with many well-known spiritual authors. There were events held at the Mayan pyramids in which rituals were being performed mixed with New Age workshops and even musical performances. So many of the New Age folks around the globe were aware of this date and they found ways to gather with others.

Yet, the media continued to play up the date as the end of the Mayan calendar signifying the end of the world. There was even a Hollywood blockbuster disaster film called *2012*. By the day after December 21, 2012, there were either people laughing that the Mayans were wrong and obviously the world never ended, or there were people who had stories about how they could feel the shift.

The truth is the world is always ending and beginning. Life is an oscillation, a reverberation through time and space. Life never ends—life just is. So as much as I enjoyed the fanfare to usher in a New Age; as much as I loved the idea that this was the new dawn for the galactic sunrise, even though I knew that cycles do end—I knew nothing was going to be any different on the morning of December 22, 2012. Was this the end of my New Age? Was I ready to become ageless?

The Bleed Out

The popularity of fasting, colon cleansing, emotional clearing, releasing negative energies and other New Age techniques are rooted in the belief that we are toxic. In addition, many New Age people are suspicious of chemicals, technology and other pollutants, and try to live as off the grid as possible. After all, a natural lifestyle is highly desired, and of course there is reason to be suspicious in a world where we are constantly exposed to new real dangers and fed deceptive information.

Modern life has been a dynamic conflict between "better living through chemistry" and "getting back to the earth." When I think about it, my platelet disorder may have some basis in being born into a chemically sterile, petroleum based, and artificially flavored world. There is no escaping it. As I have said before, "the only way out is in."

But for many New Age people the overarching fear is being gobbled up by the lower dust world. Fear of chemtrails, HAARP and other nefarious activities by the secret government's plan to eradicate the human species can pretty much lead a person to be scared to be alive. My own need to be 100% natural and my fear of drugs and surgery has brought me close to the conclusion of this story, as I came close to death in the spring of 2015. Prior to that close call, I had gone over four years with no drugs, surgery or any intervention.

Yet, my platelets were still dangerously low at all times. I remember I had been to one natural healing doctor when I was first diagnosed. He had me on several herbs and reassured me it was fine living with platelets in the teens. He had known a patient who was in single digits and chose not to get her spleen out or to take drugs. Yet four years went by and I dreaded every time I got my quarterly count. My doctor had accepted the fact that I was fine living with 90% of my platelets missing. After all, it was my choice and I was not exhibiting any of the symptoms, save the bruise here and there that would spontaneously show up on different parts of my body.

I just figured one day it would disappear. My wife and doctor did not though. My doctor was just honoring my strong wish not to be on drugs anymore or to get my spleen taken out. To me surgery was barbaric. Everything is connected in one system—everything can be healed you just have to believe! I truly knew that this was temporal and I could break through. I had even stopped eating gluten as I felt this was the root of the disorder. But deep inside I also felt like a failure, that my body was destroying itself and therefore wanting to kick me out of it.

The week before my fifth wedding anniversary I was going to get my next quarterly platelet count. I first went and had an acupuncture treatment in anticipation of receiving very high numbers. But when I got my lab results my platelets were on the borderline of being dangerously low.

    The night before when I was to take my wife up north to a hot springs resort and enjoy our anniversary getaway, I accidentally dropped my iPad off my bedside table and bruised my arm. In the morning, I woke up to find blood on my pillow. My mouth had sores in it that were bleeding and my arm was a third purple. There I was standing in the mirror colliding between two emotions—fear that my platelets were so low I would need to go to the emergency room and be hospitalized or pleasure over soaking in hot springs with my beloved wife on our anniversary and healing myself in nature. So I decided.

    Washing my mouth out and putting on a long sleeved shirt, I packed the car and north we headed! It was a great weekend in a charming cottage of our own. We soaked, read and enjoyed each other. We even hiked up to a waterfall crossing the creek several times while being very aware of our footing not to fall on the mossy rocks. At that point I may have not had enough platelets to stop any internal bleeding if I fell.

    When we got back in town after a great weekend, I began to have a stomachache. The next morning, I had blood in my stool but for some reason I figured it was not a big deal. I showered and put on some shorts and told my wife that I was going to get a kombucha—a raw probiotic drink that settles the stomach. I had called the hospital and a doctor-on-call spoke with me. I told him I was fine and felt like I just needed to walk. He said exercise and meditation is excellent—a doctor telling me to meditate?

    But when my wife saw my bloody sweat pants, she had me call the hospital again. I had minimized the whole thing. She had a vision I would be dead outside the store with my kombucha.

They wanted me there pronto so my wife fired up the Beamer and stepped on it knowing the hospital was 30 minutes away.

With my eyes tearing looking out the window as we rushed to the hospital, hiding my sadness and fear, I had become aware of the suffering I was creating for my wife by being in such denial about my body. I will always remember being the passenger to the woman who was trying to save my life, as I saw Mt. Tamalpais in the distance and the world whizzing by.

My greatest fear about my condition was the threat of internal bleeding. And now my insides were bleeding. With sores all inside my mouth bleeding, I remembered a doctor once warning me that the mouth is close to the brain and if I began cerebral hemorrhaging I could end up in a coma. That was even more worrisome than getting a platelet transfusion or a bone marrow biopsy, and yet I did not let it stop me from the bliss of soaking in hot springs.

How close was I to death? Why had I been in denial? Waves of guilt and remorse washed over me. When we finally arrived at the emergency room my platelet count was zero. I finally hit the zero-point! I could not control my body anymore. As I was hooked up to a platelet transfusion, they needed to do an upper and lower GI. I needed to drink a gallon of that stuff they make you take when you get a colonoscopy. And thus began the cleansing.

My healing crisis was a lot like my shamanic initiation. Deep cleansing, releasing everything from my gut, facing my greatest fear and instead of the guinea pig, it was me being cut open as they took out my spleen. The spleen I had been healing through herbs, energy work, talking to my cells and reprogramming my DNA. Now it was medical waste. But, I had a life lesson that would never leave me—always be aware and attend to one's body. Do not let fear deny yourself Western medical attention, it is part of a holistic approach.

All of the herbs, exercise, gluten free diet, prayer, energy work kept giving me hope that I was becoming more and more whole. Facebook friends who send me Light—they mean well. But they can't heal me. I can't heal me. The only way to truly do that is to recognize that to heal is to become whole and I am already whole—I just need to realize it.

That everything is whole because every thing is holy.

We all make the whole and everything is included. That means modern drugs too. Drugs that have possible terrible side effects but keep you alive. Side effects? There are possible side effects to living life including death and living a life in fear of death.

I still believe in many of the healing modalities I experienced and even my own system Whole Light Fusion that I have not taught for many years. As I look through my emails every morning I see dozens of invitations for all kinds of healings. Healing the soul. Healing past lives. Healing the inner child. Healing the wounded healer.

I feel the over-emphasis on healing can be quite narcissistic and self-indulgent. That is why I did not write a book that had answers to how you can heal your self, but rather questioned the fundamental nature of reality. With total acceptance of my condition and gratitude in my heart, I feel blessed and feel more alive than ever! I recognize that life is what flows through us and we are not someone who is alive but rather life itself.

I remain very open minded to all forms of healing and believe in the future we will discover how to treat the physical body at the subatomic level and correct disease without trying to change it at the physical level. I feel that spontaneous healing is very possible and may actually be some kind of anomaly similar to my zero-point *experiences*. I feel that all of my mystical experiences were little pinches to make sure I was not dreaming, or

ABOUT THE AUTHOR

I.J. Rosen was born in Brooklyn in the 1950s. Destined to live the life of the artist he moved to lower Manhattan in the late seventies and began showing in galleries and performing in underground clubs in SoHo and Tribeca. After leaving the art world, the author pursued his quest for spiritual knowledge.

From shamanic initiations in Peru with a traditional medicine man, to receiving a Masters Degree in Art Therapy—Rosen delved deeper into his own psyche. Pushing the envelope, he introduced his own form of guided imagery and self-expression into psychiatric hospitals with populations ranging from children to the criminally insane. On the other side, he developed and taught Whole Self Management programs to executives, and executive coaches in the U.S. and Australia.

I.J. Rosen is the co-author of the book *Inner Security and Infinite Wealth* (Select Books 2003) and the critically acclaimed book *The Flip* (Hampton Roads 2006). As a publisher and the founder of DreamSculpt Media, Inc. Rosen has produced dozens of digital media e-books for best selling authors, film producers and media channels as well as presented at venues ranging from the Commonwealth Club in San Francisco to TED X in Malibu. CA.

I.J. Rosen lives in the Sonoma Wine Country with his wife.

were to remind me that I am being dreamt by something much larger than my concept of Self.

I have no mystical healing conclusion to this story. No surprise ending where I wake up and realize I dreamt the entire condition, which I know I really did at some level. But I have a message for the next person who may deny all of the possibilities out there except for the ones that fit into their reality construct. Like those who could heal themselves naturally and yet choose to continually pollute their bodies in other ways.

To be truly holistic, means to be open to everything and not attached to anything. It is all a balance and you are a full spectrum being. Like a keyboard, your higher self, your Light body reality, is the high note. Physical suffering and mortality is at the low end of the keyboard. The low notes are dense matter as the high notes are spiritualized matter. We need to occupy all of it, the full scale.

When I arrived in the hospital and was told my platelet count was zero, I felt a wave of gratitude that it could not be any lower. After all, zero is the source of all power. The zero-point is like the fulcrum. It remains still yet holds the power for all movement. The outer world is a construction of my brain and nervous system and is more like a holographic projection so now I can move on in my life whether I need to be on drugs or not. Even the drugs are like a holographic projection and it's all a very detailed magic show. Yet, if I don't take that little yellow pill each day I could die—then dissolve like an ink drop in the infinite sea.

www.ingramcontent.com/pod-product-compliance
Lightning Source LLC
Chambersburg PA
CBHW071730090426
42738CB00011B/2438